W9-DIH-224

Yas - 82Z
246554

How to Read Music in 30 Days

Music Theory for Beginners - with exercises & online audio

Second Edition, © 2020 Matthew Ellul

www.SchoolofComposition.com

Published in the United States
ISBN-13: 978-1977904874
ISBN-10:1977904874

All rights reserved. No part of this publication may be reproduced, stored in a retrieval system, or transmitted in any form or by any means – electronic, mechanical, photocopying, recording, or otherwise – without prior consent of the author, except for brief excerpts or quotations in a review.

To a great teacher, Ronnie Debattista, whose music lessons unlocked a lifetime of inspiration.

Contents

PART 3. MUSICAL EXPRESSION

CONCLUSION

Preface – Read this First

Welcome to *How to Read Music in 30 Days*, I'm really glad you're here!

Would you like to know what those mystery lines and dots on the front cover mean? I'll tell you... they're the iconic *"dun dun dun dunnnn"* from Beethoven's 5th symphony. By the end of this book, you'll not only know the name of every symbol, but you'll understand exactly what each one does. By the end, you'll know how music symbols come together to create all kinds of different music that we all love.

Whether you want to compose music, write songs, play for your fans, record in a studio or anything else in music, you need to have a strong foundation in the basics – a strong understanding of how music works. This book is your practical, step-by-step guide to building that solid understanding. You'll find that some lessons are easy and quite intuitive while others might require a second reading. This is perfectly normal. As the popular saying goes:

"Every expert was once a beginner."

So, take your time with the lessons and progress at your own pace. We'll begin from absolute zero, which means that you might encounter some familiar concepts (and that's great!) but I encourage you not to skip ahead. Read through every lesson and go through the exercises so that you don't miss any important points. Later lessons build on earlier ones.

The book consists of 4 main parts:

1. From day 1 to day 15 we find out exactly how rhythm works: from basic note durations to beats, simple vs. compound time signatures, upbeats, and more;

2. From day 16 to day 24 we explore the musical alphabet: we learn all about the different musical pitches and how to notate them correctly. In these lessons we also learn about the keyboard, as it's very helpful to visualize the ideas in here.

3. From day 25 to day 29 we learn all about expression marks. These are symbols and terms that tell musicians how a note should sound. They are important for performers to understand the composer's intentions; and they're important for composers so they make their intentions as clear as possible.

4. Finally we get to day 30 - the final test, which covers every lesson we've been through.

Your Free Audio Downloads

Before we start, get your free audio downloads from *www.SchoolofComposition.com/extras*
There you'll find all the audio for the examples and the listening challenges. **If for any reason you need to contact me, send an email any time at:** *matt@schoolofcomposition.com*

How to Use this Book

Throughout the book you'll find several types of lessons:

Exercises: Every day ends with written exercises. Work them out to test your understanding of that day's lesson. The answers are available for download at _www.schoolofcomposition.com/extras_

Audio Clips: The musical examples presented throughout the lessons are available for download also at _www.schoolofcomposition.com/extras_. The examples are labelled so it's easy to find the ones you wish to listen to.

Lesson Summaries: At the end of every day, the lesson is summarized into a few bullet points. You'll find these useful later as reminders and as references of what the lessons were about.

Expert Tips & Supplemental Lessons: These are shorter articles that tackle questions that frequently come up at that point in the lesson.

Listening Challenges: These are fun activities that will help you train your ear. While the written word and the examples are very effective at showing you these ideas, these challenges allow you to listen for yourself. Music is, after all, a hearing art.

Score-reading Challenges: Here you get suggestions to listen to a composition while following along its sheet music. Instructions for what to look out for in the score are provided as well. Scores are available for free at this website: _www.imslp.org_

How to Contact the Author

If at some point during your studies you need to contact me, you can do so at: matt@schoolofcomposition.com

Let's get started! Don't forget to download the audio examples, answer to the exercises and to the final test on www.schoolofcomposition.com/extras

First Off, What is Music?

Before we begin our study of music theory and musical notation, let's define music itself. We know, of course, that music is made up of sounds. And we also know that these sounds are not usually generated at random but organized in some specific way to achieve some specific musical effect. So music is **organized sound.**

However, a good definition must not neglect the **function** of music. When a text was sung by the choirs of the Church of Ancient times, or a libretto was set to music for an Opera of the Italian Renaissance, or a composer wrote a 30 second jingle for a TV advert – music served a specific function. In other words, there is **intention** behind composing. So I hope that we can agree that one possible definition is that music is **sound organized for a purpose**.

This is exactly what this book is about. We will see **why and how musical sounds are organized** and **how** these same **sounds are notated** and represented visually.

The Significance of Music Notation

Although nowadays we are used to the idea that music is written down on paper (or presented on a screen), notation didn't appear all of sudden as a complete system. On the contrary, it has a long history of development spanning several centuries.

Before the invention of notation, music was either improvised or painstakingly learned over many repetitions imitating a master. In fact, this is how Medieval monks learned and then sang the Church hymns at religious ceremonies. Considering the vast amount of hymns that had to be sung, however, it took a significantly long time to learn them all. And accounting for human error and interpretation, there was no guarantee that a student would remember the tune exactly as it was taught to him thus making the process longer.

The first step towards a system of musical notation occurred in the 7th Century when Pope Gregory the Great ordered the codification of Christian hymns so that all of Europe could sing from the same hymnbook. The result was the first kind of music notation - a primitive set of signs and symbols known as **neums**. Neums were used to indicate the direction of the melody but they were still quite limited. It was Guido d'Arezzo, a famous Italian singing teacher of the 11th Century, who came up with the idea of representing notes on lines. He used his new system to teach music quickly to young choristers. Within a few centuries the innovative idea was developed and adopted by virtually everyone.

Guido D'Arezzo (c. 991 – c.1050)

Notation of music was a hugely important leap forward. It is responsible for the widespread influence of the Western musical tradition because music that can be written down can be saved indefinitely, transcending time and place. Its spread is no longer dependent on just word of mouth.

Moreover, writing music down meant that more complex music could be invented because creativity no longer relied solely on one person's memory. Composers could now save their musical ideas in writing and come back to them later. They could also make music for ensembles, choirs and orchestras because musicians can read music altogether.

So it is notation itself that gave rise to that special kind of musician whose job is to invent new music – that is, the composer. I hope that all of us reading this book can appreciate that when we read and write musical notation, we are connected to hundreds of years of developments by those who came before us.

Part 1. How Rhythm Works
The Two Basic Elements of Music

Whether you listen to classical, jazz, pop, rock, hip-hop, electronic or any other style, music consists of two fundamental elements: **rhythm and pitch**. Pitch is the relative frequency of notes. It's what determines how low or high musical notes are in relation to each other. On the other hand, rhythm is anything concerned with the duration and timing of notes. It's how we know when a note should be played and precisely for how long.

This simple graphic here is an illustration of these two elements. The horizontal line represents rhythm: it's that aspect of music that moves forward in time. The vertical line represents pitch: some musical notes are high, some low and others go anywhere in between. Music is made up of these two elements at the same time.

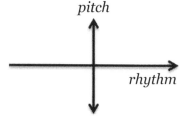

This doesn't mean that there aren't any other important factors to the creation of music. It simply means that rhythm and pitch are two of the absolute basics.

We will begin our study of music with rhythm because it is the most fundamental element. In fact, rhythm can exist without pitch but pitch cannot exist without rhythm. There are tunes that most people can recognize just by their rhythm. Try clapping the rhythm to the *Happy Birthday* tune or *Jingle Bells* to a friend – these rhythms are characteristic enough that they would probably recognize them even without the pitches – that is, without the melody.

At the same time, it's impossible to have pitch without rhythm because whenever we hear any pitch, we hear it for some amount of time (or in more musical terms: **duration**). And duration is an important topic in our exploration of rhythm.

Note: The understanding of rhythm will involve some basic math but don't let this deter you. The reward for overcoming the initial hurdles is a lifetime of enjoying music! Ask me anything at matt@schoolofcomposition.com

Day 1
Notating Rhythm

The word 'notate' is from the Latin word 'notatus' meaning 'to note down'. Musical notation is a set of symbols, markings and characters that represent rhythm, pitch and other instructions to musicians. Just like we use letters, words and sentences to communicate in everyday language, we can communicate music through notation.

The basis of musical notation is **the written note**. A note is this symbol:

It is made up of three parts: the head, the stem and the flag. By changing any of the three parts of this symbol we can notate different durations, which are better known in music as **note values**.

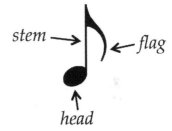

For example, this is the **Whole Note** (also known in British English terminology as the **Semibreve**):

It has neither a stem nor a flag, and its head is left empty rather than filled in. Relative to all other note values, this is the **longest**. But the exact amount of time it will be played for depends on various other factors, which we learn about later. For now, we are only concerned with the <u>relative value</u> of every note – that is, the duration of a note in comparison to all others.

In fact, all other note values derive their names in relation to the whole note. This is the **half note** (also known in British English as the **minim**) and its duration is **half the whole note**:

This means that the duration of 2 half notes is equal to 1 whole note: ♩ + ♩ = o

Next is the **quarter note** (in British known as the **crotchet**). The symbol is similar to the half note except that the head is filled in. Its value is of **a quarter of a whole note**:

And so the duration of 4 quarter notes are equal to the duration of 1 whole note.

Next comes the **eighth note** (also known as the **quaver**). Its relative duration is that of an eighth of a whole note. The symbol is similar to the quarter note but with the addition of the flag:

And of course, 8 eighth notes are equal to one whole note:

Next comes the **sixteenth note** (also known as the **semiquaver**). Its relative duration is that of a sixteenth of a whole note. It looks similar to the eighth note except for the addition of a second flag:

And 16 sixteenth notes are equal in duration to 1 whole note:

In theory this pattern can go on indefinitely. If we were to discuss the next note, it would be half the duration of the previous one and the symbol would have an added flag. The note after that would be half yet again and its symbol would have yet another flag and so on and on.

Thirty-second note:
(or demisemiquaver)

Sixty-fourth note:
(or hemidemisemiquaver)

We'll get into all the detail of how these work in music step-by-step in the coming lessons. For now, just keep in mind that <u>the value of these notes in relation to each other never changes</u>.

One way of seeing this is to imagine a pie. If the full pie is the whole note, then half of it is a half note. If we split each half into two again, we get four quarter notes. Split them again and we get 8 equal parts (8 eighth notes) and so on, every time dividing by half.

1 whole note / 1 semibreve

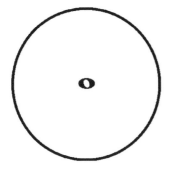

2 half notes / 2 minims

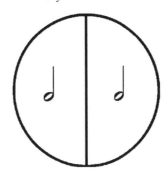

4 quarter notes / 4 crotchets

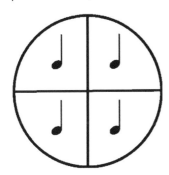

8 eighth notes / 8 quavers

Note Values Summary Chart

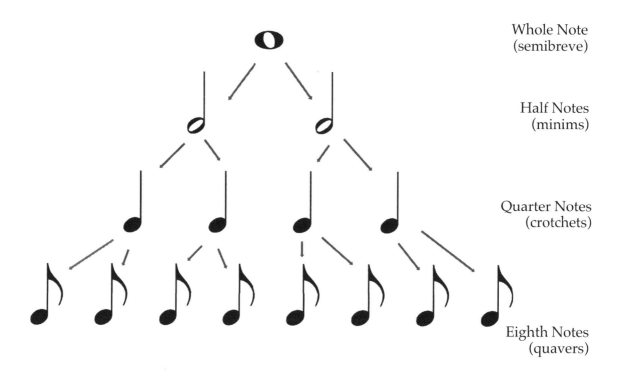

Whole Note
(semibreve)

Half Notes
(minims)

Quarter Notes
(crotchets)

Eighth Notes
(quavers)

Sixteenth note:

Thirty-second note:

Sixty-fourth note:

ⓘ Expert Tip: How to Memorize Note Value Symbols

Here's a little exercise that will help you remember the symbols and their names.

Look at the chart of note values on the this page and notice that from any note value to the one directly below it, the symbol has just one addition to it.

For example, for a whole note to become a half note, simply add the stem. For a half note to become a quarter note, simply fill in its head.

In other words, we only **add one thing** to the note value to get the next symbol – the symbol that is half the value of the previous one. *That one thing is either a stem, coloring in the head or adding a flag.*

Of course, this works in reverse as well. To double the note value (that is, to go up to the next note value in the chart) we **take away one thing** from it. For example, take away the flag from an eighth note and you get a quarter note.

Try this exercise on a separate sheet of paper. Draw a whole note and 1) Add a stem, 2) Color in its head, 3) Add a flag and 4) Add in a second flag. In four steps you went from a whole note to a sixteenth note. Now do it also in reverse, draw a sixteenth note and change it into a whole note one step at a time. Write in pencil so that you can erase and adjust easily.

Exercises for Day 1

1. The typical written note is made up of 3 parts. One of these is the head. What are the other two?

   a. ___Stem___

   b. ___flag___

2. This first note is a whole note. What are the other note values called?

   𝐨 = *whole note*

   ♩ = ___half note___

   ♩ = ___quarter___

   ♪ = ___eighth___

   ♬ = ___sixteenth___

3. Write:

   a. A whole note: 𝐨

   b. A quarter note: ♩

   c. A sixteenth note: ♬

   d. A half note: ♩

   e. An eighth note: ♪

4. Fill in the blanks in each of these statements.

        a. The whole note is equal to _two_ half notes.

        b. The whole note is equal to _____ quarter notes.

        c. The quarter note is equal to_____ eighth notes.

        d. The quarter note is equal to_____ sixteenth notes.

        e. The half note is equal to _____ eighth notes.

        f. The half note is equal to _____ quarter notes.

        g. The half note is equal to _____ sixteenth notes.

5. Answer these note value sums by writing another note. The first one is done as an example.

a. ♪ + ♪ = ♩

b. ♬ + ♬ + ♬ + ♬ =

c. ♩ + ♬ + ♬ + ♬ + ♬ =

d. ♩ + ♩ =

e. ♪ + ♬ + ♬ =

f. ♩ + ♪ + ♪ + ♩ + ♪ + ♪ =

g. ♩ + ♩ + ♩ =

h. ♩ + ♪ + ♪ + ♪ + ♪ =

i. ♩ + ♬ + ♬ + ♪ + ♬ + ♬ + ♪ =

8

Day 2
The Musical Pulse

So far we've seen the relative durations of the **note values**. We know, for example, that a half note is half the whole note and also double the quarter note. We know also that the quarter note is half the half note as well as double the eighth note and so on.

But how do we know the duration of these notes in real time? How do we decide how short or long a note should actually be played for?

For this we need a more complete picture of rhythm and an important part of it is **the musical pulse**. This is one aspect of how we measure musical time. The pulse is that constant, underlying throb that is felt in music as it plays along. It's often referred to simply as 'the beat'. It's what people tap their feet to when listening to a song.

Here's a basic visual representation of a pulse. It's just a simple row of squares but observe that they're equal in size and they're always the same distance apart. This is because the pulse is **steady**, **consistent** and all the beats are **the same duration**:

Now to measure musical time accurately, we have to decide **what these beats are worth**. And to do this we must **assign a note value to the pulse**. So instead of squares, we'll put a note value, let's say for example, quarter notes. Here we have a **quarter note pulse** where every beat is a quarter note.

This is useful because now that we know that 1 beat is 1 quarter note, we can measure how many beats every other note value is worth. (We can do this because we already know the relative durations of our note values from day 1.) If the quarter note is **one beat**, then the whole note is 4 beats, the half note is 2 beats, the eighth note is one-half of a beat and the sixteenth note is one-fourth of a beat.

Note Value	Quarter note beat
Sixteenth note	one fourth of a beat
Eighth note	one half of a beat
Quarter note	one beat
Half note	two beats
Whole note	four beats

Later in the course we'll see how rhythms are built on top of the pulse but here's a simple demonstration. This is a short quarter note pulse:

What can we do with it?

We can build rhythms above it using note values! For example, on top of the first two quarter notes we can put one half note. *(To download these examples visit www.schoolofcomposition.com/extras)*

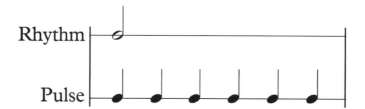

Audio Example 2.1

On the next four quarter notes, we can put one whole note:

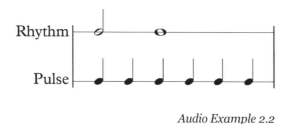

Audio Example 2.2

Or another half note and two quarter notes:

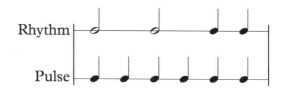

Audio Example 2.3

As we explore rhythm throughout this book, you'll see that the variety is endless! When we add pitches to rhythms, we get melodies, bass lines, accompaniments and other musical features. Underneath it all, there is always this constant musical pulse.

┌───┐

Day 2 Quick Summary

♫ *The pulse is the constant underlying beat.*

♫ *The pulse is steady and consistent.*

♫ *The pulse is assigned a note value (quarter note, half note, eight note, etc.) so that it becomes a 'quarter note pulse' or a 'half note pulse', 'eighth note pulse' and so on.*

♫ *The rhythms of melodies and accompaniments are built on top of a pulse.*

└───┘

Exercises for Day 2

1. Answer *true* or *false* to the following statements.

   a. The **relative** durations of notes are always the same. For example, the half note is always half the whole note.

   b. The musical pulse is always changing.

   c. The pulse must be assigned a unit of measurement (such as the quarter note).

2. If one beat equals **one** quarter note:

   a.   The whole note is worth _____ beat/s.
   b.   The half note is worth _____ beat/s.
   c.   The quarter note is worth _____ beat/s.
   d.   The eighth note is worth _____ beat/s.
   e.   The sixteenth note is worth _____ beat/s.

3. Compose two simple rhythms of your choice on top of the quarter note pulses.

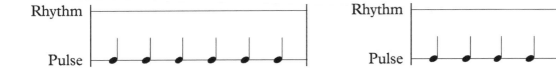

Day 3
Tempo

Students often assume that 1 beat takes 1 second of clock time but this is a mistake. When we created a quarter note pulse in the last lesson, we did **not** conclude that one beat would be played for any specific number of seconds. The actual time it takes to play a beat is determined by **Tempo**. The word *tempo* is the musical term for pace (or speed) – if the tempo is quick, the beats are shorter (because they are closer together) and if the tempo is slower, the beats are longer (because they are further apart from each other).

The plural of *'tempo'* is either *'tempi'* or *'tempos'*.

Before we proceed, please keep in mind that tempo **doesn't** affect the relative durations of the notes – for example, the half note is still and always will be twice as long as the quarter note no matter how fast or slow they are played.

Tempo Terms, the Metronome & Beats per minute

To indicate what the tempo is, composers write specific musical terms at the beginning of the music. As from the Romantic era (c.1810 to 1910), composers used terms in their own languages, but in earlier times it was traditional to use terms in Italian. This is because Italy was the place where Classical music began to flourish back in the Renaissance.

These terms are still in use today. For example, the Italian word *Allegro* is an indication that the music should be played quickly. And the term *Lento* is Italian for *slow*. A problem that arises with these terms, however, is that although we know that *Allegro* means *'quickly'* and *'Lento'* means *'slowly'*, we don't really know exactly how quick or how slow.

Johann Maelzel (1772 – 1838) solved this problem with the invention of **the metronome**. The job of his device is to make a click sound (or a beep if it's a modern electronic or digital version) at any tempo we choose. Every one of those clicks represents a beat and so it makes an audible pulse.

The metronome measures speed in **'beats per minute'** – shortened to *'bpm'*.

> *Sound clips mentioned here are available for download at*
> *www.schoolofcomposition.com/extras*

Let's get a quick feel for the difference between two different tempos. Listen to *audio example 3.1*: this is 120 beats per minute on the metronome. Now listen to *audio example 3.2*: this is a composition by Mozart played at around this same tempo.

Now compare that to the tempo of 70 bpm on the metronome – *audio example 3.3*. And listen to the 2nd movement of the same piece by Mozart played around the same tempo: *audio example 3.4*. As you can hear, tempo is a significant influence on the character of the music.

Common Tempo Markings

Here is a table of the 6 most common Italian terms for tempo, their meaning and their equivalent beats per minute.

Italian term	*Meaning*	*Bpm*
Largo	Very slow and broad	40
Adagio	Slow	60
Andante	At a walking pace	80
Moderato	Moderately	100
Allegro	Lively and quick	120
Vivace	Very fast	140

Note that in practice, these terms represent a range of tempos and not strictly one speed. *Adagio* is listed as 60 bpm but it could also be 54 or 68 bpm. *Allegro* is listed as 120 bpm but it could also be 116 or 126 bpm. The exact tempo always depends on context. You can hear examples of this anytime you listen to the same piece played by different musicians – the tempos vary according to their interpretation of the composer's ideas.

Notating the Metronome Mark

For a tempo marking to be accurate, it's not enough to know the amount of beats per minute. We also need to know what those beats are worth. Are they quarter note beats? Half note beats? Eighth note beats? Something else? In the last lesson we learned that the pulse consists of recurring beats and that those beats must be assigned a note value.

So the complete marking of tempo consists of two parts: first, the value of each beat (such as quarter notes or half notes) and second, by the number of beats per minute.

For example, here we have *"100 quarter note beats per minute"*. This means that the pulse consists of quarter notes and there are exactly 100 of them in a minute.

Here is another example. This one is *"80 half note beats per minute"*. It means that the pulse consists of half notes and there are exactly 80 of them in a minute.

$$\quarternote = 100$$

$$\halfnote = 80$$

```
┌─────────────────────────────────────────────────────────┐
│                  Day 3 Quick Summary                     │
│                                                          │
│  ♫ Tempo is the pace (or speed) of a composition.        │
│                                                          │
│  ♫ Tempo is indicated by specific musical terms,         │
│     traditionally in Italian.                            │
│                                                          │
│  ♫ Tempo can be measured accurately with 'beats per      │
│     minute' (bpm).                                       │
└─────────────────────────────────────────────────────────┘
```

👂 Listening Challenge: **What Tempo Is It?**

Here's a list of 12 pieces of music by different composers from different eras. Your task is to download and listen to the music at *www.schoolofcomposition.com/extras* and work out what the tempo of each piece might be.

Choose the tempos from the 6 common terms we learned in this lesson:

Largo, Adagio, Andante, Moderato, Allegro and *Vivace.*

> *Whether you get them right or wrong is not as important. The purpose of this task is get you to listen to the effect that tempo has on music.*

1. Mendelssohn: Symphony no. 1, 3rd movement: *Allegro*

2. Vivaldi: Op. 3 no. 5, RV519: 2nd movement: _____

3. Beethoven: Sonata for Violin and Piano no. 5, 'Spring':   _____

4. Albinoni: Concerto a Cinque no. 11 Op. 10:   _____

5. Rachmaninov: Piano Concerto no. 2, Op. 18, 1st movement: _____

6. Corelli: Concerto Grosso no. 3, Op. 6, 4th movement: _____

7. Paganini: Caprice no. 10, Op. 1:   _____

8. Mozart: Sonata for Piano, K. 545 2nd movement: _____

9. Bizet: Symphony no. 1, 2nd movement: _____

10. Bach: Brandenburg Concerto BWV 1046, 2nd movement: _____

Exercises for Day 3

1. Answer true of false to these statements:

a. One beat is always one second of clock time.

b. If the Tempo is quicker, the beats are shorter and they are closer together.

c. If the Tempo is slower, the beats are longer and they are further apart from each other.

d. Tempo does not affect the relative durations of the notes. Those are always the same.

2. What does *Bpm* stand for? _____

3. What is the function of the metronome? _____

_____

_____

4. Choose the correct translation of these Italian terms. (*Choose from: Very fast; Moderately; Slow; Very Slow and broad; At a Walking Pace; Lively and quickly*).

Next to the translation also write an estimate of each ones' beats per minute.

       a. Andante   _____ ; _____ Bpm

       b. Allegro   _____ ; _____ Bpm

       c. Vivace   _____ ; _____ Bpm

       d. Moderato   _____ ; _____ Bpm

       e. Largo   _____ ; _____ Bpm

       f. Adagio   _____ ; _____ Bpm

Day 4
Meter, Time & Beats

Meter is **the division of beats into equal groups**.

Here is a pulse made up of 6 quarter notes:

Although it's quite simple, it can be played in various ways. Let's try one possibility where the 6 quarter notes are divided into 2 groups of 3 quarter notes.

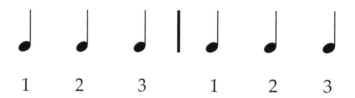

1   2   3   1   2   3

Audio Example 4.1

Now let's try a different one. This time the pulse is divided into 3 groups of 2 quarter notes:

1   2   1   2   1   2

Audio Example 4.2

I'm sure we agree that these pulses are very different in their musical effect. <u>But how did we distinguish that these two are different at all?</u>

The answer is in the **accents**. Just like in everyday language where some words are more stressed than others, in music some beats are stronger than others (or we can say, some beats are **accented**).

In the first example above, the 6 quarter notes are divided into 2 groups of **3 beats each**. The first beat of every group is stronger than the other two – it is accented. And so we perceive the meter as being **'in three'** meaning that the pulse has a recurring *'one, two, three, one, two, three, etc.'* effect. Another term for 'in three' is to say that the meter is 'triple'.

In the second example, the strong beat appeared every 2 beats and so we perceive the meter to be 'in two' – its effect is of a recurring *'one, two, one, two, etc.'*, where the 'one' is strong (accented) and the 'two' is weaker. Another term for 'in two' is 'duple meter'.

These cycles of strong and weak beats are better known in music as **meters**. They can be in any amount of beats but the most common are the ones in two (or duple meters), in three (or triple meters) and four (or quadruple meters).

In musical notation these groups of beats are organized into **measures** (also known as **bars**) and separated by **bar lines.**

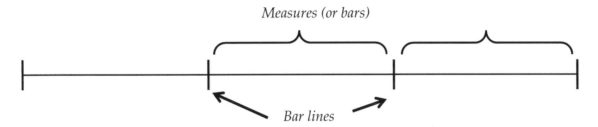

Measures (or bars)

Bar lines

Time Signature

To indicate the meter quickly and clearly in musical notation, we use **Time Signatures**. A time signature consists of two numbers, one sitting on top of the other:

In sheet music you'll find a time signature at the beginning of the music. Here's an example from a song by Schubert:

So, what do these numbers mean?

The number on top tells us **the amount of beats per measure**. It tells us whether the meter is in two, three, four or more. The time signature 2/4 shows us that the meter is in two; there are two beats in every measure.

The bottom number tells us **what those beats are worth**. It shows us whether the beats are eighth notes, quarter notes, half notes, or any other note value.

This bottom number is relative to the whole note. The easiest way to work out what the beats are worth is to divide the whole note by that bottom number. For example, if the bottom number is a 2, work out 'a whole note divided by 2' and that results in two half notes. So when the bottom number of a time signature is a 2, the beats are half note beats.

What about a four as the bottom number? The whole note divided into 4 gives us 4 quarter notes. So a time signature with 4 as the bottom number represents a quarter note pulse.

Bottom Number	Beat
1	whole note beat
2	half note beat
4	quarter note beat
8	eighth note beat
16	sixteenth note beat
and so on.	

So the time signature two-four indicates that the meter is 2 quarter beats per measure. This is a **duple meter,** which means that it's made of two recurring beats – the first beat is the strongest, the second being the weaker. *Examples of music in these time signatures are also at: www.schoolofcomposition.com/extras. Listen to Example 4.3 for a composition in two-four meter.*

> *Note that the time signature is not a math fraction although it does look like it. This is why we do not say 'two fourths' but simply 'two-four'. In this book, time signatures are referred to by the numbers connected by a dash (-), such as the 'two-four'.*

Let's look at another example. This is the time signature three-eight:

Audio Example 4.4

Since the top number is a three, then we know that this meter consists of 3 beats per measure. It is a **triple meter.** Now we need to figure out what kind of beats they are. Since the bottom number is an eight, then they are eighth notes.

Three-eight is a triple meter of **3 eighth note beats per measure**.

And what about the time signature two-two:

Audio Example 4.5

The number on top tells us that there are two beats per measure. What kind of beats? The bottom number, also a two, indicates that they are half note beats. So this meter is a **duple meter** and it consists of **two half note beats per measure**.

Now try it out for yourself. Before we move on, define this time signature:

$$\frac{4}{4}$$

4 quarter note beats for each measure

Answer

The bottom number tells us that the beat is a quarter note beat. How many quarter note beats per measure? From the top number we know that it's four. So this is a **quadruple** meter that consists of **four quarter note beats per measure**.

You might have noticed that some time signatures are very similar. For example, two-two and four-four both hold the same amount of notes in a measure, and two-four and two-two are both duple meters. We'll discuss this issue in more depth at a later stage.

Strong & Weak Beats (Accents)

As we've mentioned, meters are made up of a fixed layout of strong and weak beats. However, don't let the words *'strong'* and *'weak'* mislead you. They are terms that allow us to explain this particular aspect of rhythm. There is nothing better with strong beats, or worse with weak beats. They are both equally important. It is with these two together that meter works. (*Indeed, the strong beats wouldn't be strong at all if we didn't have the weaker ones to compare them with.*)

In duple meters, the first beat is the strongest while the second is weak. The example here is in two-four meter but the same applies to any duple meter such as two-eight or two-two.

In the following diagrams, S stands for strong and w stands for weak.

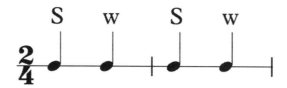

Audio Example 4.2

In triple meters, the first beat is the strong and it is followed by two weak beats.

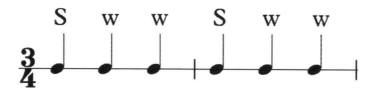

Audio Example 4.1

In quadruple meters, the first and third beat are strong and the second and fourth are weak. The first beat, however, is stronger than the third so the four beats are: Strongest, weak, strong, weak.

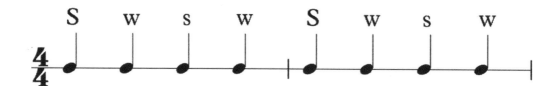

Audio Example 4.6

It's important to note that these strong and weak beats are not forced by musicians – they occur naturally within melodies, chord progressions, accompaniments and so on because music is naturally made up of patterns.

At the same time, the impression of strong and weak beats of a meter is often altered according to the flow of the music. A strong beat can be felt earlier or later than expected. In fact, this is a common way of giving the music a sense of variety. We'll see some examples of this in day 15 but for now it's important to understand this theoretical outline of strong and weak beats.

So what can we do with this knowledge of meters? Let's take that last time signature as an example and compose a rhythm. Here we have four empty measures of four-four time:

From our discussion of time signatures, we know that there are four beats per measure and each of those beats is worth a quarter note. Let's fill our first measure with 4 quarter notes:

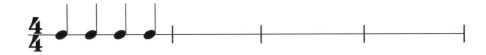

We know, also, that two quarter notes equal one half note so we can fill the next measure with two half notes.

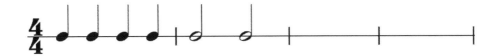

For the next measure, let's mix it up. We'll fill the first two beats with a quarter note each and we'll fill the rest of the measure (two beats) with a half note:

Now let's finish with a long note. Since one whole note is equal to four quarter notes, the whole note can fill up an entire measure in this meter. Our four-measure rhythm is complete:

Audio Example 4.7

And that is one possibility out of many, many more. Try it out for yourself on a separate sheet using the same meter. Now it's important to note that here we've worked it out backwards. We chose a meter and filled it in with a rhythm. In practice, it's the character of the music that dictates what the meter is. However this exercise is fun and helpful to understand the concept of meter and how it works.

Day 4 Quick Summary

♫ *Meter is the division of beats into equal measures (a.k.a. bars) & separated by bar lines.*

♫ *Meter is indicated by the time signature at the beginning of the music.*

♫ *In theory, the first beat of every measure is the strongest one.*

◉ Listening Challenge 1: **Is it a March or a Waltz?**

Here's a list of 10 compositions by a variety of composers. Your task is to download and listen to the sound clips at *www.schoolofcomposition.com/extras* and write whether the piece is a March or a Waltz.

Marches are in **duple meters**, most typically in two-four and sometimes two-two. Waltzes are in **triple meters**, normally in three-four but sometimes also in three-two and three-eight. Whether you get them right or wrong is not so important. The purpose of this task is to get you to listen to the difference between duple and triple meters.

> **Hint:** *Marches have a duple 'one – two – one – two' effect that corresponds to marching: 'left – right – left - right'. Waltzes have a triple 'one – two – three –one – two – three' effect that is common in music that accompanies dancing. Waltzes have an 'oom – pah – pah – oom – pah - pah' effect.*

Next to the composers' names, write whether the clip is a March or a Waltz:

1. Strauss: _____   6. Tchaikovsky: _____

2. Schubert: _____   7. Strauss Junior: _____

3. Chopin: _____   8. Offenbach: _____

4. Beethoven: _____   9. Debussy: _____

5. Tchaikovsky: _____   10. Sibelius: _____

👂 Listening Challenge 2: **Is it a Duple or a Triple meter?**

If you've enjoyed the previous challenge, here's another one that is slightly more demanding. Your task is to download and listen to the sound clips at *www.schoolofcomposition.com/extras*. Then write whether the piece is in a duple or a triple meter.

This is slightly more challenging than the previous one because not all duple meters are marches and not all triple meters are waltzes.

> *Once again it's not that important whether you get them right or wrong. The purpose is to get you to listen to the difference between duple and triple meters.*

Next to the composers' names, write whether the clip is in duple meter or in triple meter:

1. Bach: _____   6. Handel: _____

2. Beethoven: _____   7. Haydn: _____

3. Bach: _____   8. Haydn: _____

4. Dvorak: _____   9. Paganini: _____

5. Grieg: _____   10. Waldteufel: _____

Exercises for Day 4

1. Finish these statements:

    a. Meter is the division of beats into _equal groups_.

    b. We can hear where the divisions occur because the first beat of every group is _accented_.

    c. To say that a rhythm is *in three* is to say that the strong beat occurs every _third beat_.

    d. Groups of beats are written inside bars or measures. These measures are separated by _Bar lines_.

    e. In music notation, meter is indicated by the time _signature_.

f. And it is made up of 2 numbers: the one on top shows us the number of
~~bpm~~ *bpm* ; the number at the bottom shows us _beat worth_ ;

2. Define these time signatures. *(Follow the example.)*

a. $\frac{2}{4}$ _____ *two quarter note beats per measure* _____.

b. $\frac{3}{8}$ three ~~eighth~~ *eighth* notes per measure

c. $\frac{2}{2}$ ~~two~~ 2 half note beat.

d. $\frac{4}{4}$ 4 quarter note beats .

e. $\frac{3}{4}$ 3 quarter note beats .

3. Indicate the layout of each time signature's strong and weak beats. *(Follow the example)*.

a. $\frac{2}{4}$ _____ *Strong, weak* _____.

d. $\frac{4}{4}$ s, w, s, w .

b. $\frac{3}{8}$ Strong, weak, weak.

e. $\frac{3}{4}$ s, w, w .

c. $\frac{2}{2}$ strong, weak ~~weak beat~~ .

4. Put in the correct time signature before each line of rhythm below:

a.

b.

c.

5. Complete these measures by writing **one note** at the places marked *.

a.

b.

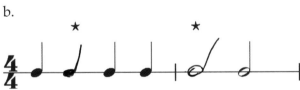

c.

d.

Day 5
The Sound of Silence

For every note value, we have an equivalent **rest**. Rests are symbols that represent a silent duration. These are important because musicians must know precisely not only when and what to play but also when to stop and for how long.

Here is a table of the note values and their equivalent rests:

	Note Value	Equivalent Rest
Whole	𝅝	—
Half	𝅗𝅥	—
Quarter	𝅘𝅥	𝄽
Eighth	𝅘𝅥𝅮	𝄾
Sixteenth	𝅘𝅥𝅯	𝄿

Just like note values, the pattern for rests can go on. If we were to discuss the next rest, it would be half the sixteenth note and its symbol would have an additional flag. The rest after that would be half yet again and its symbol would have yet another flag:

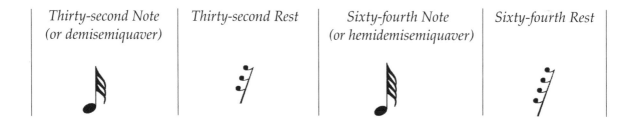

Thirty-second Note (or demisemiquaver)	*Thirty-second Rest*	*Sixty-fourth Note (or hemidemisemiquaver)*	*Sixty-fourth Rest*

Following is a simple example of rests in use. The rhythm consists of two measures of four-four meter. Notice the various rests that are part of it and notice also that they (the silences) are just as important as the actual notes.

Audio Example 5.1

One last thing before we conclude this short lesson is that there is one exceptional use of the whole rest: if a measure is empty (that is, silent), it's filled with the whole rest no matter what the meter is. In these instances, it is known as the **whole bar rest**.

whole bar rest

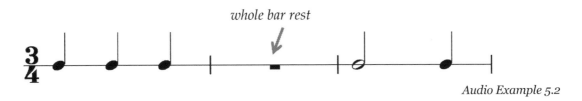

Audio Example 5.2

Day 5 Quick Summary

♫ *In music, silence is measured with rests.*

♫ *For every note value, there is an equivalent rest.*

Exercises for Day 5

1. Rests are used to measure and indicate ____Silence____.

2. Write:

    a. A quarter rest: d. A half rest:

    b. A sixteenth rest: e. An eighth rest:

    c. A whole rest:

3. Work out these sums using **rests only.** *(The first one is done for you.)*

    a.   𝄾 + 𝄾 = 𝄽

27

b. γ + γ + γ + γ =

c. ξ + γ + γ + γ + γ =

d. ▬ + ▬ =

e. γ + γ + γ =

f. ξ + γ + γ + ξ + γ + γ =

g. ξ + ξ + ▬ =

h. ▬ + γ + γ + γ + γ =

i. γ + γ + γ + γ + γ + γ + γ + γ =

4. Complete these measures by putting **one rest** at the places marked with this sign: *.

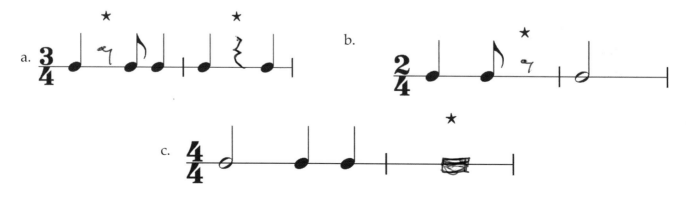

28

ⓘ Supplemental Lesson
Recap: How Rhythm Works

Now that we've looked at the basic elements one by one, let's put them together and review exactly how rhythm works. Before we begin, review days 1 through 5 if you have any doubts about the basic note values and their equivalent rests.

There are four basic components to rhythm: Pulse, Tempo, Accent and Subdivisions.

1. **Pulse:** This is the constant, underlying beat that people tap their feet to when listening to a song.

2. **Tempo:** The pulse can be played fast, slow or anywhere in between. Tempo is the pace (or speed) of the music.

3. **Accent:** Some beats are more emphasized than others. This is not forced by musicians but happens naturally as music falls into patterns.

4. **Subdivision:** On top of the pulse, we get melodies and chords that are made up of a variety of durations (note values and rests).

Here's how it all comes together in written music. The circled numbers are explained below the diagram.

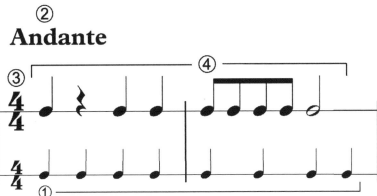

① This is a visual representation of the **pulse**. It's a cycle of equal beats. Every one of these beats is the same length: in this case, they're all quarter notes *(crotchets)*. Please note that this is for visualization purposes only; the pulse is not shown in real sheet music.

② The word *Andante* is one out of hundreds of **tempo** indications in various languages. This particular one is Italian and it translates to '*At a walking pace*'. This music should be performed neither slow nor fast but somewhere in between.

③ These numbers are the time signature. It specifies how the pulse is grouped into equal measures. The number on top indicates **how many beats there are in every measure** (in this example, four) while the number at the bottom indicates **what the value of the beats are** (in this example also four, which means quarter notes).

This pulse, therefore, is made up of <u>four quarter note beats per measure</u>. These recurring cycles of four quarter note beats can be felt because the first beat of every measure is **accented**.

Notice also that the measures are separated by bar lines.

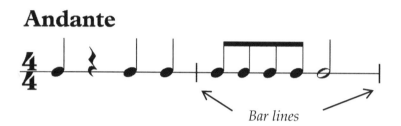

④ On top of it all, the rhythm is composed of a variety of **subdivisions** of the beat. In this example, we have quarter notes, eighth notes (joined with a beam), a half note as well as a quarter rest.

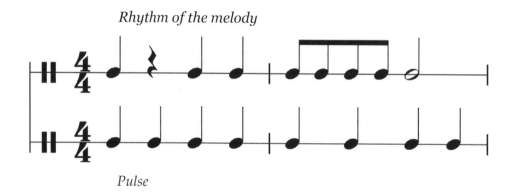

Day 6
Adding Duration with the Rhythm Dot

With a dot placed directly to the right of a note head, the duration of that note increases by half its original value.

Let's see an example. This is a dotted half note:

The half note alone is equal to 2 quarter notes. The dot is worth half of that: 1 quarter note. So, in total, **the dotted half note is equal to 3 quarter notes** – 2 from the original half note and 1 from its dot.

What about a dotted whole note?

We know the whole note is equal to 2 half notes. The dot adds half this original value, that is: one half note. So the dotted whole note is equal to three half notes (two from the whole note itself, and one from its dot). At the same time, of course, every half note is equal to 2 quarter notes each so in total, the dotted whole note is also equal to 6 quarter notes.

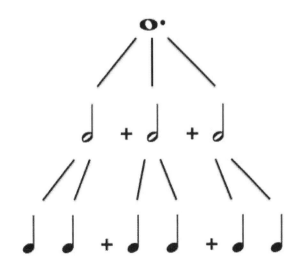

Think about the rhythm dot just like the English word "half." In the phrase "A year and a half", the word "half" means six months. But in the phrase "A month and a half", the word "half" now means only two weeks. The rhythm dot works exactly in the same way. Its exact value depends on what comes before it.

Let's work out 2 more examples. This note is a dotted quarter note.

The quarter note is equal to 2 eighth notes. The dot adds another eighth note (half the original). In total, the dotted quarter note is equal to three eighth notes.

$$ \text{♩.} = \text{♪} + \text{♪} + \text{♪} $$

Finally, let's work out the dotted eighth note. The eighth note is equal to two sixteenth notes. The dot adds another sixteenth note because that's half the original and so in total, the dotted eighth note is worth three sixteenth notes.

$$ \text{♪.} = \text{♬} + \text{♬} + \text{♬} $$

The rhythm dot applies exactly the same way to rests. A dotted whole rest, for example, is worth three half rests. And a dotted half rest is equal to three quarter rests.

Here is a table of dotted note values and their equivalent in rests.

	Dotted Note	Equivalent Rest
whole	𝅝•	▬•
half	𝅗𝅥•	▬•
quarter	♩•	𝄽•
eighth	♪•	𝄾•

Following is an example of a rhythm from Tchaikovsky's *Morning Prayer* from his *Children's Album Op. 39.* The dotted notes are important – they contribute to the overall musical character.

Audio Example 6.1

Here is that same rhythm with the pulse shown underneath. The rhythm on top is the original rhythm of the melody. The one below is the pulse outlining the three quarter beats per measure of three-four meter.

Rhythm of the melody

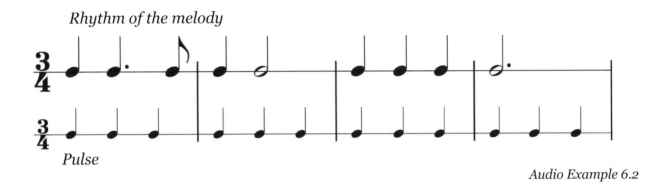

Pulse

Audio Example 6.2

The Double Dot

Although its use is not as common as the single dot, the duration of a dotted note can be extended by the addition of a second dot. This second dot will be worth **half the duration of the first dot**.

A double dotted half note, for example is equal to a half note plus a quarter note plus an eighth note:

$$\text{𝅗𝅥}.. = \text{𝅗𝅥} + \text{♩} + \text{♪}$$

Day 6 Quick Summary

♫ *The dot adds half the value to the original note.*

♫ *The dot can be applied to all notes and all rests.*

♫ *The double dot extends the duration of a dotted note. The second dot is worth half the first dot.*

Exercises for Day 6

1. Explain in brief what the rhythm dot does: _____ .

2. This first note is a dotted quarter note. What are the others?

a. 𝅘𝅥• = _____*dotted quarter note*_____ .

b. 𝄽• = _____

c. 𝄾• = _____

d. 𝄻• = _____

e. 𝅘𝅥𝅮• = _____

f. 𝅝• = _____

3. Draw:

    a. A dotted whole note: d. A dotted half note:

    b. A dotted quarter rest: e. A dotted eighth note:

    c. A dotted half rest:

4. Fill in the blanks in each of these statements.

    a. The dotted whole note is equal to three *half notes.*

    b. The dotted eighth note is equal to three _____

    c. The dotted quarter note is equal to three _____

    d. The dotted half note is equal to three _____

5. Work out these sums by writing **one dotted note**.

a. ♪ + ♪ + ♪ = ♩.

b. ♬ + ♬ + ♬ + ♬ + ♬ + ♬ =

c. ♩ + ♬ + ♬ + ♩. =

d. ♩ + ♩ + ♩ =

e. ♪ + ♬ + ♬ + ♬ + ♬ =

f. ♩ + ♪ + ♪ + ♩ =

g. ♩ + ♩ + ♩ + ♩. =

h. ♪ + ♪ + ♪ + ♪ + ♪ + ♪ =

i. ♬ + ♬ + ♬ =

j. ♪ + ♪ + ♩ =

k. ♪ + ♬ =

l. o + ♪ + ♪ + ♪ + ♪ =

Day 7
Adding Duration with the Tie

Although the dot is useful to increase the duration of note values, it is also limited because as we've seen, it increases the duration of the note **specifically by half its original value**.

A more flexible means of adding to the duration of a note is by **tying** it to another note. **A tie is a curved line strung between 2 notes.** The tied note is not struck, played or sung again; instead, its duration is added unto the original so that it is prolonged.

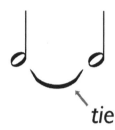

Here's an example of a simple rhythm without ties. *All sound clips are downloadable at* *www.schoolofcomposition.com/extras*

Audio Example 7.1

Now here it is with a tie. Listen to how the tied note is not played again but its duration is added unto the first note instead.

Audio Example 7.2

The tie is useful in 3 particular cases:

1. **Adding notes together over a bar line:** Since it is not possible to have note durations longer than one full measure in any meter, we can use  the tie to create longer notes. In the example here, the meter is in 3, but thanks to the tie, the note is 6 quarter notes long – the equivalent of 2 full measures in this meter.

2. **Adding notes together to produce a specific duration:** Often we might need to have a note duration that is not possible using standard note values only. In the first example below, the resulting duration is of a quarter note plus a sixteenth. There is no way of notating such a note value other than with the tie. The same goes for the second example. There's no way of notating the specific duration of a half note plus an eighth note except for with the tie.

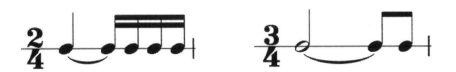

> *The flags of eight notes and smaller notes are grouped into beams to make notation easier to read. We discuss this in detail on Day 10.*

3. **Adding 3 or more notes together:** The tie is not limited to 2 notes. It can be used over as many notes or measures as are needed. In this example, we have a long note made up of three notes tied together:

It is interesting to see that **dotted notes can be written also as tied notes**. These 2 rhythms on the right sound exactly the same! We still use dotted notes, however – they are standard practice and musicians are used to them. Musical notation also tends to be less cluttered using dots instead of ties when possible.

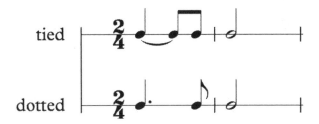

Example 7.3

Day 7 Quick Summary

♫ *The tie adds together the duration of two or more notes.*

♫ *A tied note is not struck or played again; its duration is added on to the first note.*

Exercises for Day 7

1. A tie is a curved line strung between two notes. What is its purpose?

_____

_____

_____.

2. Assuming that the quarter note is assigned the value of 1, what is the combined value of each set of tied notes? *(The first one has been done as an example. Some answers require fractions.)*

a.  = 5

b.  =

c.  =

d.  =

3. Rewrite these dotted notes as two equal tied notes.

a. **O•**

b.

c. **♩.**

d.

Day 8
More Time Signatures

So far we've mostly seen meters where the pulse is measured in quarter note beats. In this lesson we take look at meters (and their time signatures) where either the eighth note or the half note is the beat.

The Eighth Note Beat

We've learned already that when the pulse consists of quarter note beats, the bottom number of the time signature is 4. Now, when the pulse consists of **eighth note** beats, the bottom number of the time signature is **8**.

As always, the top number of the time signature shows us the amount of beats per measure. The bottom number shows us what each of those beats are worth – in this case, eighth notes. So the time signature two-eight means that we get *2 eighth note beats in every measure.*

Similarly, these are 3 eighth note beats per measure, and 4 eighth note beats per measure:

The table here shows how the note values relate to different kinds of beats. The quickest way of calculating these proportions is to keep in mind **which note value is assigned the value of 1.**

The sixteenth note, for example, is one fourth of a beat if the beat is a quarter note. In other words, when the quarter note equals 'one', the sixteenth note equals 'one-fourth'. But when the beat is an eighth note, then that same sixteenth note

Note	Quarter Note Beat	Eighth Note Beat
Sixteenth	One fourth	One half
Eighth	One half	**One**
Quarter	**One**	Two
Half	Two	Four
Whole	Four	Eight

becomes half a beat. That is, if the eighth note equals 'one', the sixteenth note equals 'one-half'.

The Half Note Beat

Now let's look at meters where the pulse consists of half note beats. In the time signature, half note beats are indicated with a number 2 at the bottom.

For example, this is three-two meter.

The bottom number is 2 so the meter consists of half note beats. How many half note beats per measure? According to the number on top: 3. So this time signature is '**3 half note beats per measure**'

Similarly, these are 2 half note beats per measure and 4 half note beats per measure:

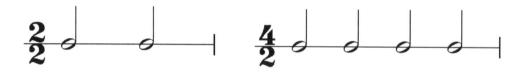

Just as before, our note durations acquire a different value depending on the beat. So if the quarter note equals 'one beat', then it takes two eighth notes to fill one beat. But if the half note equals 'one beat', then it takes four eighth notes to fill one beat.

Note	Quarter Note Beat	Half Note Beat
Sixteenth	One fourth	One eight
Eighth	One half	One fourth
Quarter	**One**	One half
Half	Two	**One**
Whole	Four	Two

Day 8 Quick Summary

♫ *The pulse (or the beat) can be assigned any note value: half note, quarter note, eighth note and so on. Any note value can be designated as 'one beat'.*

♫ *When the meter consists of half note beats, the bottom number of the time signature is 2.*

♫ *When the meter consists of eighth note beats, the bottom number of the time signature is 8.*

What can we do with these time signatures?

We can compose rhythms! Let's start with a simple rhythm in three-eight. This meter consists of **three eighth note beats per measure** so let's have the pulse clearly mapped out. For this exercise we'll use four measures:

Now let's compose a simple rhythm on top. How about a quarter note followed by an eighth note for the first measure?

That works. Any ideas for the second measure? We can have a dotted quarter note that fills up the whole measure; or perhaps three eighth notes for a more lively rhythm. Another good possibility is to repeat the first measure:

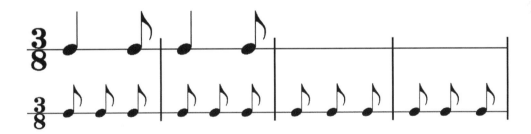

For the third measure let's have a long note:

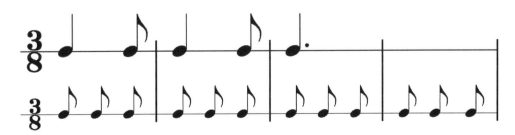

And to finish off we'll have an eighth rest followed by a quarter note:

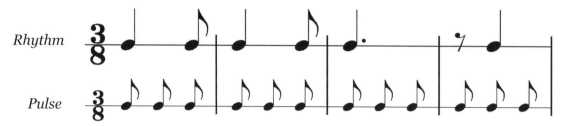

Example 8 .1

That's our complete rhythm in three-eighth. Of course the possibilities are endless – this is just one out of many! *(Don't forget to go listen to the final rhythm at www.schoolofcomposition.com/extras when you get the chance!)*

Let's compose another rhythm. This time we'll use the simple duple meter two-two. Like before, we'll map out the pulse – **two quarter note beats per measure**:

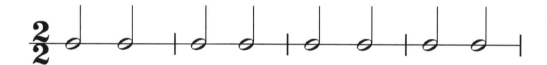

Let's begin with the first measure. How about a dotted half note followed by a quarter note? (we didn't use any dotted notes in the other rhythm):

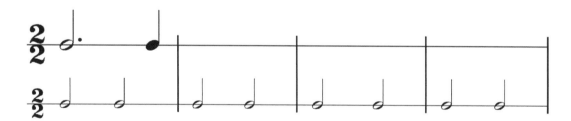

As before, we have endless possibilities for the second, third and fourth measure but let's keep it simple. Let's have a half note followed by 2 quarter notes in the second measure:

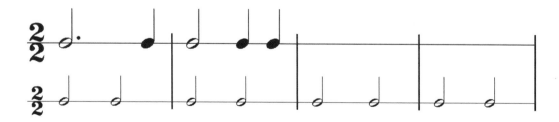

For the third measure, we can do the opposite of the second measure: 2 quarter notes first and then a half note.

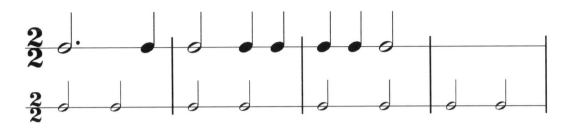

And we'll finish off this rhythm with a long note that fills up the entire measure: a whole note.

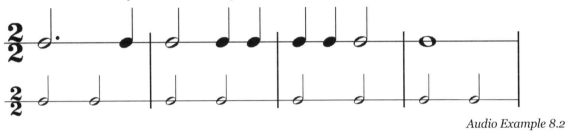

Audio Example 8.2

Note that here we've worked out rhythms backwards – we started out with a time signature and we slowly put in a rhythm that fits. Outside of practice, it's the character of the rhythm itself that tells us what the time signature should be. There's also no need to work on one measure at a time – a rhythmic pattern could very well take up half a measure, two measures and half or any other amount.

Exercises for Day 8

1. When the **eighth note** equals one, what is the value of each of these notes?

    a. A quarter note: *2*

    b. A whole note: _____

    c. An eighth note: _____

    d. A sixteenth note: _____

    e. A half note: _____

2. When the **half note** equals one, what is the value of each of these notes:

    a. A half note: *1*

    b. An eighth note: _____

    c. A sixteenth note: _____

    d. A whole note: _____

    e. A quarter note: _____

Day 9
Simple vs. Compound Meter

As we learned about meters and time signatures throughout this book, we described them as duple (2 beats per measure), triple (3 beats per measure) or quadruple (4 beats per measure).

But apart from duple, triple or quadruple, time signatures are also categorized as either **simple** or **compound**. This distinction is important because of the musical qualities inherent in these types of meter.

Simple time signatures are those that we've covered so far. What makes them *simple* is that each beat of the meter is **naturally divisible by 2** (whereas we'll see that compound meters are naturally divisible by 3). For example, two-four is a simple meter because every quarter note beat is naturally divisible by 2:

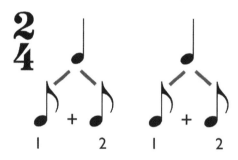

So the time signature can be categorized as a **simple duple meter**.

---

*The term '**naturally divisible**' is important because later we'll make a distinction with '**artificial division**' of the beat.*

Another simple duple meter is two-two. It is duple because it's made up of 2 beats per measure and it is simple because each of those beats is naturally divisible by 2.

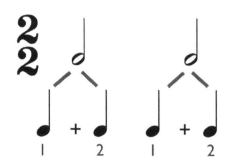

Compound Meter

For every simple meter, there is a compound meter counterpart. While simple meters are those whose beats are naturally divisible by 2, every beat in a compound meter is **naturally divisible by 3**.

Here's how this works: the simple duple meter two-four is made up of 2 quarter note pulses per measure and each of those is naturally divisible into two eighth notes.

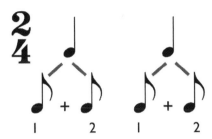

But if the meter was made up of **2 dotted quarter notes** instead, each of these 2 pulses are now **naturally divisible into 3** equal parts:

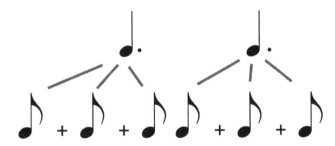

In fact, the time signature for a meter made up of 2 dotted quarter notes is six-eight – **6 eighth note beats per measure.**

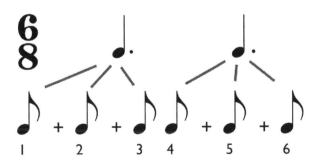

45

Keep in mind, however, that **the main beats are still the two dotted quarter notes**. To distinguish between these main beats and their divisions, we can use the words **'pulse'** and **'subdivisions'**.

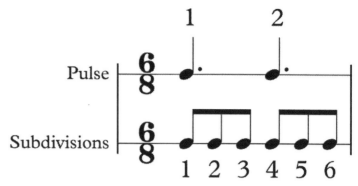

And as usual, the first of these two pulses is strong and the second is weak.

So six-eight is a duple meter. Since each of the 2 beats is naturally divisible by 3, it is compound. The full description of the time signature six-eight is: **Compound Duple Meter.**

Let's look at another example. This is a simple triple meter made up of **3 eighth notes per measure.**

Its compound triple counterpart must consist of **3 dotted eighth notes per measure** and each of the 3 dotted eighth notes are themselves divisible by 3:

Adding those divisions up (the sixteenth notes) we learn that the time signature of this meter is nine-sixteen. Since the pulse is in 3, this time signature is **compound triple.**

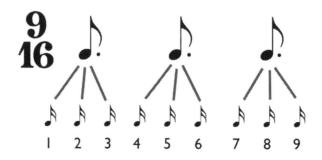

Finally, let's look at an example of a compound quadruple meter. This measure is filled with 4 dotted half notes. What is the time signature?

Let's get to the answer step-by-step. Every dotted half note can be broken down into 3 quarter notes:

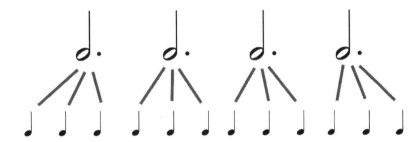

The measure is now filled with 12 quarter notes. The top number of the time signature will therefore be 12. The bottom number must represent the quarter note subdivision and from our experience with simple meters we know that this is 4.

So the time signature of this compound quadruple meter is **twelve-four**. The pulse is in 4 and each one is divisible into 3 quarter notes:

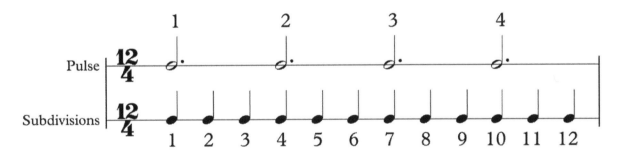

Day 9 Quick Summary

♫ Meters can be categorized as simple or compound.

♫ Simple meters are those whose beats are naturally divisible by two.

♫ Compound meters are those whose beats are naturally divisible by three.

ⓘ Supplemental Lesson
Why 6/8 is not 3/4

At this point in the course, students often ask about time signatures that seem very similar:

- *What's the difference between the time signatures 6/8 and 3/4? They both hold 6 eighth notes per measure.*
- *Why bother with the time signature two-two if we have four-four? They both hold four quarter notes per measure.*
- *What's the difference between two-four meter and two-two? They're both simple duple meters.*

Let's tackle these questions one by one. The difference between the time signatures 6/8 and 3/4 is in the accents. 3/4 is three quarter note beats per measure:

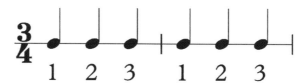

Whereas 6/8 is two dotted quarter note beats per measure:

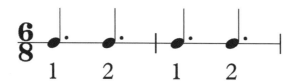

Although they can both hold six eighth notes in every measure, the effect is completely different because of where the beats are. Six-eight consists of 2 groups of 3 eighth notes:

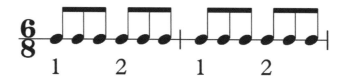

while three-four consists of 3 groups of 2 eight notes:

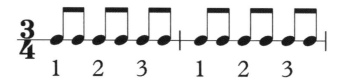

48

This is why the distinction between simple and compound time signatures is important. Six-eight is **compound duple** while three-four is **simple triple**. The musical characters (or we can say '*the qualities*') of these meters are entirely different even though they are mathematically equal. You'll hear examples of these differences in the listening challenge at the end of today's lesson.

Two-two and four-four are different for similar reasons. While two-two is a **duple meter**, four-four is a **quadruple meter**. In other words, two-two consists of two beats per measure – a '*one-two one-two*' recurring effect:

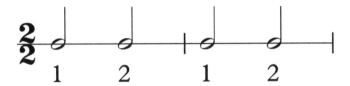

while four-four consists of a '*one-two-three-four one-two-three-four*' effect'. It's made up of four beats per measure:

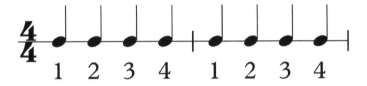

This is the same reason why two-four and four-four are different. Two-four often has a very clear '*one-two one-two*' effect that is typical of marches. Four-four, on the other hand, typically comprises longer melodic and rhythmic patterns.

Having said that, the difference between these two meters is sometimes vague. There are plenty of examples where music can be rewritten into the other meter without affecting it at all. Professional musicians know how to bring out the proper character of the music whatever the time signature is.

That brings us to the last question – the difference between two-two and two-four. *What's the use if they're both simple duple?*

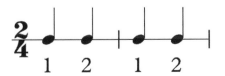   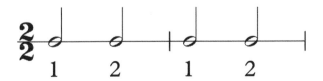

The difference between these two is often a matter of making the notation easier to read. Let's say we have this rhythm in two-four:

Since it's full of very small subdivisions (eighths, sixteenths and smaller), it will be more reader-friendly if all note values where doubled. This transforms the time signature from two-four into two-two and is easier to read:

Now consider this rhythm in two-two:

This rhythm is full of long notes (half notes and above) and so at first glance it gives us the impression that it is somewhat slow. The tempo marking, however, contradicts this, as it is actually quite fast (132 half notes per minute).

It makes sense to rewrite this rhythm in two-four by dividing all the note values by half. Now the rhythm consists of shorter notes and looks closer to what it actually sounds like. *(Later in the course we learn how to double or halve a rhythm without changing how it sounds).*

In conclusion, the important difference between meters is in their quality: are they compound, simple or something else such as complex? Are they duple, triple, quadruple or more? When meters share the same quality – for example two-two and two-four are both simple duple meters – then it's a matter of making the notation easier to read. Keep in mind that musical notation is a system of communicating through symbols – the process of music making is smoother if those symbols are clear to understand.

Table of Time Signatures

	Simple	*Compound*
Duple	2/8 2/4 2/2	6/16 6/8 6/4
Triple	3/8 3/4 3/2	9/16 9/8 9/4
Quadruple	4/8 4/4 4/2	12/16 12/8 12/4

This symbol is an alternative to 4/4: **C**

This symbol is an alternative to 2/2: **¢**

Recognizing Simple vs. Compound Time Signatures

Although these are not all commonly used, the table on the previous page reveals how time signatures are related to each other. Notice that all simple meters have 2, 3 or 4 as the top number, whereas compound meters have 6, 9 or 12 (numbers divisible by 3).

Notice also that to transform a Simple Time Signature to a Compound Time Signature we can simply multiply the top number by 3 and the bottom number by 2.

Traditionally, the most common meters in use are 2/4, 2/2, 3/8, 3/4, 4/4, 6/8 and 9/8. Contemporary classical, jazz and rock music tend to make a lot more use of complex meters, which we'll discuss on Day 11.

𝔇 Listening Challenge: **Is it Simple or Compound?**

In this listening challenge, your task is to determine whether the musical extract is in a simple meter or a compound meter. *As usual the sound clips are available at www.schoolofcomposition.com/extras*.

> *Once again, it's not that important whether you get these questions right or wrong. The purpose is to get you to listen to the difference between simple and compound meters.*

Next to the composers' names, write whether the musical extract is in **simple** meter or **compound** meter:

1 - Marcello: _____   7 – Prokofiev: _____

2 - Mussorgsky: _____   8 - Smetana: _____

3 - Lehar: _____   9 - Beethoven: _____

4 - Mozart: _____   10 – Vaughan Williams:

5 - Gounod: _____   _____

6 – Offenbach: _____

1. Simple meters are those whose beats are naturally divisible by _____.

2. Compound meters are those whose beats are naturally divisible by _____.

3. Identify these meters as *simple duple, simple triple, simple quadruple, compound duple, compound triple or compound quadruple.*

a. $\frac{2}{2}$ _____   f. $\frac{4}{4}$ _____

b. $\frac{6}{8}$ _____   g. $\frac{3}{8}$ _____

c. $\frac{2}{4}$ _____   h. $\frac{9}{8}$ _____

d. $\frac{6}{4}$ _____   i. $\frac{3}{4}$ _____

e. $\frac{9}{16}$ _____   j. $\frac{12}{4}$ _____

Day 10
Grouping

To help make notation easier to read, the flags of eighth notes and notes of smaller value are joined together. For example, this rhythm:

is much easier to read than this one, even though they sound the same:

Grouping means that the flags of the notes become beams – horizontal lines that join the notes. In fact, another word for 'grouping' is 'beaming'. The rule for grouping notes is simple: **group together notes that make one beat**. Here are some examples. This one is in four-four:

In two-four:

In six-eight:

And three-four:

There are some nuances to beaming that make notation even easier to read. Here's a list of suggestions to follow – there's no need to memorize them – just use this list as a guide.

1. When the first and/or last two beats in four-four meter consist of eighth notes only, they are grouped together:

2. At the same time, beams never exceed the value of a half note (in four-four meter).

3. Note values that are smaller than the eighth note are normally beamed in groups of one quarter note at a time:

4. Beams always begin on the stronger (or strongest) beat **unless the group is preceded by a dotted note or a rest**:

5. If eighth notes fill a measure of two-four, three-four or three-eight time signatures, they are normally beamed as shown:

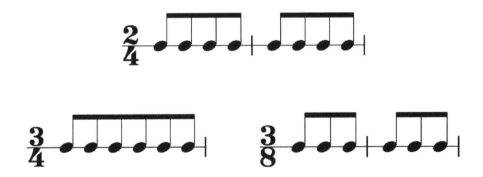

While these are standard groupings, composers sometimes deviate and group notes in unorthodox ways to help show the character of the music better. But it's important to be familiar with the typical groupings in order to recognize any deviations.

Day 10 Quick Summary

♫ To make notation easier to read, eighth notes and smaller note values are joined with a beam that replaces their flags.

♫ Notes are beamed in a way that shows where the beats of the meter are.

♫ Long groups of several beats begin on a strong beat unless the group is preceded by a dotted note or a rest.

Exercises for Day 10

1. On a separate sheet of paper, rewrite these rhythms so that all eighth and sixteenth notes are grouped correctly according to their meter:

Day 11
Complex Meter

The final kind of meters that we'll discuss is **complex meters**. These meters do not fit in the simple or compound categories because they are a mixture of both. One measure of complex time signature consists of two or more pulses of different lengths.

A common complex meter is the **quintuple meter** five-four: <u>5 quarter note beats per measure</u>:

Typically, this meter has **2 stronger pulses.** Unlike simple and compound time signatures however, the pulses are **not the same.** Instead, the 5 beats are divided into a group of 3 and another of 2:

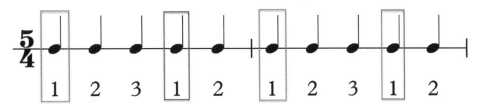

Audio Example 11.1

This strong-weak pattern of five-four is: **Strongest, weak, weak, Strong, weak**

Another possibility is a group of 2 beats followed by a group of 3. The strong beats here occur on the first and the third quarter note beats.

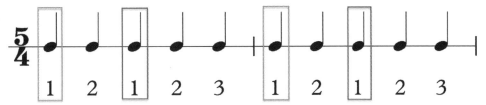

Audio Example 11.2

The strong-weak pattern here is: **Strongest, weak, Strong, weak, weak**

This combination of groups of twos and threes is what makes the meter **complex**. Obviously, the rhythms composed in complex meters have different characters and possibilities than those in simple and compound meters. *(But this doesn't mean that complex meters are better – they're just different!)*

One of the first major composers to use this quintuple meter was Tchaikovsky in the 2nd movement of his 6th symphony.

Example 11.3 – Rhythm only
Example 11.4 – Original piece

> *The 3 on top of the 3 eighth notes of measures 1 and 3 are **triplets** and they are explained fully in the next lesson.*

Let's take a look at a **septuple meter** (that is, a meter made of 7 beats). This is seven-eight: 7 eighth note beats per measure.

Audio Example 11.5

As we've said, complex meters are most often a mixture of duple and triple. This meter is no different and the 7 eighth notes are organized into 2 duple pulses and 1 triple pulse. This gives us 3 possibilities of organizing the 7 beats. The first is like the diagram above shows: 3 + 2 + 2. Another possibility is 2 + 2 + 3:

Audio Example 11.6

And finally, 2 + 3 + 2:

Audio Example 11.7

Day 11 Quick Summary

♫ *Complex meters are neither simple nor compound but a mixture of both.*

♫ *The strong pulses of complex meters are not equal (in length and duration) but a mixture of twos and threes.*

Exercises for Day 11

1. How are complex meters different from simple and compound meters?

_____

_____

_____

2. Complete these rhythms in any way you like. Provide 2 solutions to each one. *There are no wrong answers here as long as your measures are filled with the right number of beats.*

a.

b.

c.

d.

e.

f.

Day 12
Tuplets, Duplets, Triplets

In our discussion of simple and compound time signatures we learned that the difference between them is whether the individual beats are naturally divisible by 2 (simple meters) or naturally divisible by 3 (compound meters):

However, it's also possible to divide a beat by 3 in a simple meter and to divide a beat by 2 in a compound meter. This is a kind of artificial division of the beat and it's notated by what is known as **tuplets**. A tuplet is **a subdivision of a note into a number that is not normally permitted by the meter.**

The Triplet

By far the most common tuplet is the **triplet**. The triplet is used in simple meters and it allows the **division of a note into 3 equal parts** instead of the normal 2.

Here's an example. This is a simple rhythm in two-four:

Audio Example 12.1

Here, the second pair of eighth notes of the first measure is transformed into a triplet: three eighth notes in the time of two. Listen to the examples and notice that the triplet is simply dividing the quarter note beat into three equal parts.

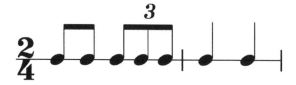

Audio Example 12.2

In order to make the notation clear, the notes that make up the triplet are beamed together with a small number 3 in the middle.

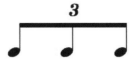

If the notes cannot be beamed together (because they don't have flags such as quarter notes or bigger), a bracket with a small number 3 makes it clear:

When you listen to the examples you might feel that the triplet is played faster. This occurs not because the tempo changes but because we're putting in more notes in the same space (to fit, they must be shorter).

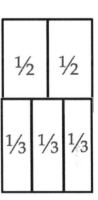

In example 12.1 the quarter note is divided into 2 while in example 12.2, that same quarter note is divided into 3.

Always keep mind that a triplet is **3 of one type of note played in the same amount of time as 2 of that same type.** For example, 3 <u>quarter</u> notes in the time of two <u>quarter</u> notes or 3 <u>eighth</u> notes in the time of two <u>eighth</u> notes.

The Duplet

Another common type of tuplet is the **duplet**.

The duplet is the opposite of the triplet. It's **the division of a note into 2 equal parts (instead of the normal 3).**

In compound meter, the natural subdivisions of each dotted beat is into 3 eighth notes (3 equal parts). Listen to the example and notice that the duplet simply divides the beat into two (instead of three):

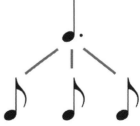

In this example in 6/8, the duplet allows us to artificially divide the dotted quarter note into 2 parts instead of 3:

Audio Example 12.3

61

Notice the notation with the small number 2 indicating the duplet. The duplet is always **2 of one type of note played in the same amount of time as 3 of that same type.**

Note: *do not confuse the terms tuplet and duplet. Tuplet refers to the whole category of artificial subdivisions of a note. A **duplet** is a specific type of tuplet that is 2 notes played in the time of 3.*

While the triplet and the duplet are the most common of artificial divisions, there are countless other possibilities.

We can have **quintuplets** (subdivision into 5 equal parts), **sextuplets** (a subdivision into 6 equal parts) and **septuplets** (subdivisions into 7 equal parts), just to name a few.

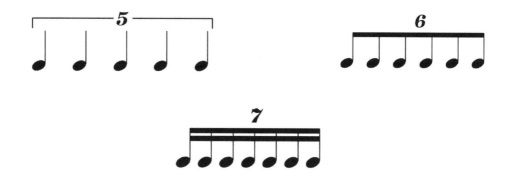

Day 12 Quick Summary

♫ *Tuplets allow the subdivisions of beats (or parts of beats) into an amount that is not normally permitted by the meter.*

♫ *A triplet is the division of a note into three equal parts instead of the normal two (used in simple meters).*

♫ *A duplet is the division of a note into two equal parts instead of the normal three (used in compound meters).*

We said that the triplet is the division of a note into three equal parts instead of two. But we can use those three equal parts in different ways. Here we'll discuss some examples.

Let's begin with a simple rhythm that contains a triplet of eighth notes:

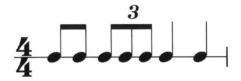

Audio Example 12.4

Now here is that same rhythm with the triplet changed into a quarter and an eighth note. The triplet here is worth exactly the same amount as before (one quarter note) because it's still the subdivision into **three equal parts**. The difference is that the quarter note takes two of those parts and the eighth note takes the third part:

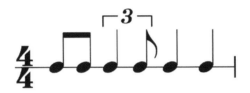

Audio Example 12.5

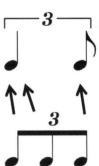

Here's another example. This time the triplet contains a dotted rhythm:

Audio Example 12.6

And finally, the triplet here contains a rest:

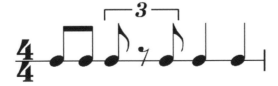

Audio Example 12.7

In all these examples the notes still add up to a triplet of eighth notes (which in turn add up to one quarter beat). The point of this short lesson is that the actual rhythm of a triplet doesn't always show three equal parts.

The triplet creates the space for the subdivision into three parts, but those parts can be handled in various ways. And this applies to all tuplets.

Exercises for Day 12

1. Fill in these measures in various meters by adding a triplet or a duplet at the places marked *. The first is done as an example.

64

Day 13
Playing Around with Time Signatures

In this lesson we're going to play around with meters so that we'll strengthen our understanding of it.

To begin, we'll rewrite meters and their rhythms as double or half of the original without changing the way they sound.

The main idea behind rewriting any meter is that **notes must keep their relative value in their meters**. So a note that is worth <u>one beat</u> in one meter will still be worth <u>one beat</u> in the new meter. A note that is worth <u>half a beat</u> in one meter will still be worth <u>half a beat</u> in the new meter and so on.

Doubling & Halving Meters

Let's say we have this rhythm in two-four:

What would the meter be if we doubled the value of every note?

At first thought, many assume that the double of two-four would be four-four. Although it's mathematically correct that a measure of four-four can hold double the amount of beats as two-four, rhythmically and musically it's not quite correct.

The character of a meter depends on its pattern of strong and weak beats. In the case of two four, a strong beat occurs every two quarter beats (and so we say that it is **in two** or that it is **duple**). But with the time signature of four-four, the pattern is different. The strongest beat occurs every four quarter beats.

In order to double the meter without changing the character of the rhythm, the new time signature must also be in two; and a measue must also be double the value. The time signature that fulfils these criteria is two-two. While two-four holds **two quarter** notes per measure, two-two holds **two half** notes per measure.

So, the doubling of our original rhythm will look like this:

Now what about halving the original? Just as before, we need a time signature that fulfils two criteria: it must be in two just like the original, and a measure must hold half the amount of beats. The time signature that fulfils these criteria is two-eight: two eighth note beats per measure.

So halving the original rhythm will look like this:

At this point you might be wondering how it can be that these rhythms sound the same.

- *Isn't the one in two-eight faster than the one in two-four?*
- *Isn't the one in two-two slower than the one in two-four?*

This is now a question of **tempo**. Let's say the tempo of the original rhythm in two-four is 120 **quarter** note beats per minute. *What should the tempo of the other two rhythms be so that they sound the same as the original?* The answer is quite simple:

Since the rhythm in two-four is measured in **quarter note beats** and there are 120 of them in a minute, then the tempo of the rhythm in two-two will be 120 **half note beats** per minute because that meter is measured in half notes.

is the same as

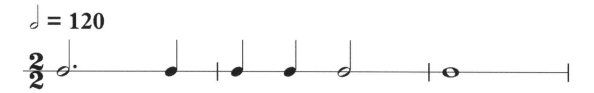

and the same as

These rhythms sound exactly the same because they consist of the same number of beats per minute and the relative subdivisions are the same. For example, the last measure in the two-four rhythm is a half note (two beats) whereas the last measure in the two-two rhythm is a whole note (also two beats in its meter).

This is an important lesson: meters, rhythms and tempos are relative to each other and once we can manipulate the notation of rhythm however we like.

Rewriting Simple & Compound

Apart from doubling and halving, it's also possible to rewrite a rhythm from a simple meter to a compound meter (and vice versa) without changing the way it sounds.

As we will see, tuplets will come in handy in such an exercise because we will need to control the subdivisions of beats in order to maintain exactly the same rhythm between simple and compound.

Let's try an example. This rhythm is in simple three-four meter:

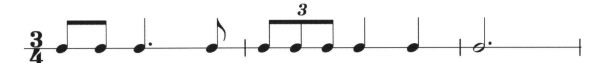

Adapted from Haydn's Minuet of Piano Sonata No. 28

How do we rewrite this into a compound meter? In order to maintain its melodic and rhythmic character, the new meter must also be a triple one. In our previous lessons we saw that a measure in three-four time could quite easily become a measure in nine-eight time if we just add a dot to each beat:

Since it turns out that nine-eight and three-four are related, we can rewrite the rhythm in nine-eight meter. Let's begin with the triplet units. These are normal in compound meter and so we can just rewrite them as they are. Notice that they are no longer considered *'triplets'* because they are not 'three notes in the time of two'. Units of three are absolutely normal in compound meters.

Next let's consider the quarter notes of the original. In three-four meter, any one quarter note takes up one whole beat. In order to maintain the rhythm's character, these notes should be rewritten so that they still take up a whole beat in the new meter. Since one beat in nine-eight meter is a dotted quarter, **the quarter notes in three-four meter become dotted quarter notes in nine-eight meter**.

The same principle can apply to the dotted half note in the last measure. This note takes up 3 beats, (the whole measure in three-four meter). The only way to have one note fill up a whole measure in nine-eight is by tying a dotted quarter note to a dotted half note:

What is left is the first measure. And it consists of pairs of eighth notes. As we know from previous lessons, the only way to subdivide a beat of a compound time signature into two equal halves is by using the duplet. So here's the complete rhythm:

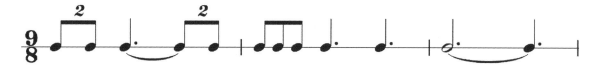

From Compound to Simple

Now let's go through a similar exercise in the opposite direction: from compound to simple. Here we have a rhythm in six-eight:

Adapted from Ravel's Daphnis and Chloe, Danse General

As we know, six-eight is a compound duple meter. So the extract will be rewritten in a simple duple meter. Remember that to maintain its character, we must maintain the original **duple** effect. In other words, the new meter must also be **in two**.

Which simple duple meter shall we use? Removing the dots from the dotted quarter notes of six-eight beats results in two-four so that is our answer:

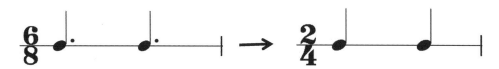

Since they both consist of two beats per measure, two-four and six-eight are related.

Let's begin by rewriting the simplest notes. As we've learned, any note that takes up one beat in compound meter will be rewritten as a note that takes up one beat in simple meter too. This will maintain the character of the rhythm.

Notice that the final note of the original (a dotted half note that fills up the last measure) is rewritten as a half note (and it fills up the last measure of the new meter).

To finish, we need to rewrite the groups of three eighth notes from the original nine-eight to the new two-four. As we've seen before, the only way to subdivide a beat of a simple meter into three equal parts is by employing the triplet.

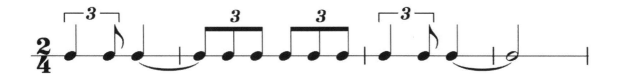

Day 13 Quick Summary

♫ *Rhythms can be rewritten in different meters without changing how they sound.*

♫ *Meters can be halved and doubled as well as transformed from simple to compound or compound to simple.*

Exercises for Day 13

1. On a separate sheet of paper, double the following meters and their rhythms.

a.

b.

c.

d.

2. On a separate sheet of paper, halve the following meters and their rhythms.

a.

b.

c.

d.

3. Rewrite this simple meter into compound meters *(hint: you'll need duplets)*.

a.

4. Rewrite this compound meters into simple meter *(hint: you'll need triplets)*.

a.

Day 14
The Upbeat

It's rather common for a rhythm to begin on a weak beat or a weak part of a beat. This is known as an upbeat: **a note, or group of notes, that precede/s the first strong beat.** The upbeat acts as a kind of springboard that leads into the strong beat. Another term for strong beat, in fact, is **downbeat**.

For example, in the popular *Happy Birthday* tune, the first strong beat is on the syllable *Birth* (first part of the word *Birthday*) – the rhythm of the word *Happy* is the upbeat.

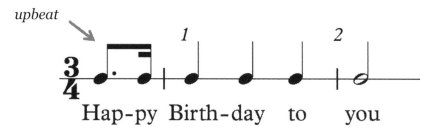

Audio Example 14.1

Notice that the upbeat makes up an **incomplete** measure. When we number our measures, the incomplete measure is not counted as measure number one. **Measure one is the first full measure.**

The beginning of Charpentier's *Te Deum*, usually played by the trumpet, is a very well-known tune that begins on an upbeat:

Audio Example 14.2

Here is another example. This one is from Boccherini's popular Minuet from *String Quintet No. 5*. In this case the upbeat consists of a group of 4 sixteenth notes:

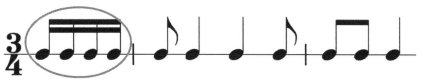

Audio Example 14.3

72

In Op. 28 no.7, Chopin constructs a short and sweet prelude using only this rhythm:

Audio Example 14.4

Since the same two-measure rhythm is repeated another 7 times, each occurrence of the rhythm ends on the second beat of its measure. The third beat, then, becomes the upbeat of the next occurrence of the rhythm.

upbeat

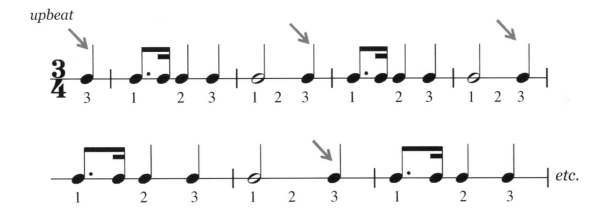

Notice how this means that the upbeat can be used anywhere within a piece and not just the very beginning. In the Chopin example, the upbeat is a significant feature of the music's character so it makes sense that once employed, it reappears over and over again.

The full score of Chopin's Prelude is on the following page. For ease of reading, the rhythm alone is copied on the first line and the original piano score is given underneath.

The full piece is listed as Audio Example 14.5 in your downloads from:
www.schoolofcomposition.com/extras

Prelude
Op. 28 no. 7

F. Chopin

| Day 14 Quick Summary |

♫ *Any notes that precede, and lead into, the strong beat are known as an upbeat.*

♫ *Upbeats can occur anywhere in the music, not just the beginning.*

👂 Listening Challenge: **Is that an Upbeat?**

Music that begins on an upbeat is very common and you'll get used to the feel of an upbeat just by listening to many examples. In this challenge you'll find a list of 10 musical extracts. Your task is to determine whether the clip begins on an upbeat or not.

All sound clips are available for download at: www.schoolofcomposition.com/extras

1. Beethoven: Sonata for Violin & Piano No. 3, Rondo _____

2. Away in a Manger (Christmas Traditional): _____

3. Chopin: Nocturne Op. 9 No. 2 _____

4. Bach: Cello Suite no. 1 'Prelude': _____

5. Dvorak: Tempo di Valse _____

6. Haydn: Sonata 59 'Finale': _____

7. Handel: Sarabande: _____

8. Albeniz – Asturias: _____

Exercises for Day 14

1. Add an upbeat of your choice to these rhythms. *(There are no wrong answers here. Just keep them simple and remember that upbeats can consist of several notes and not only one).*

Day 15
Syncopation

Back in Day 4 we learned that every meter has a set pattern of strong and weak beats. However, the rhythm of music doesn't always follow that expected pattern. It often happens that the strong beat is felt earlier or later than expected. This creates a kind of a rhythmic jolt as the rhythm disrupts our expectation of a strong beat. The effect is known as **syncopation**.

Syncopation occurs when a note that is on a weak part of its measure is made stronger than its surrounding notes: either by lengthening it more than the other notes (giving it what we can refer to as *'rhythmic weight'* or by accenting it (that is, making it louder).

The rhythm below is from Scott Joplin's tune *The Entertainer*. The marked notes are syncopations because they occur on a weak beat and they're longer than any other notes around them. **The effect is as if the strong beats occur earlier or later than expected.**

Audio Example 15.1 & 15.2: Joplin: The Entertainer

For a syncopated rhythm to be effective the meter and its pulse should have already been made clear; otherwise there wouldn't be anything to disrupt. The surprise of interrupting the pulse is impossible without it being predictable first.

Notice also that the melodic phrase ends on a normal strong beat at the beginning of the fourth measure. The rhythm relaxes momentarily as it finally reaches a strong beat that coincides with the strong-weak patterns of its meter.

In this next example, Beethoven syncopates the rhythm simply by instructing the pianist to make the second beat louder than the first (in the 2nd and 3rd measures).

The indication *sf* is short for *Sforzando*, which is Italian for *'with force'*. This is an example of syncopation because the accented notes are on the second beat of their measures. In two-four meter, these beats are usually the weaker ones.

Audio Example15.3: Beethoven: Piano Sonata No. 13 Allegro Vivace, measures 119 – 122

┌───┐
│   │
│   *Day 15 Quick Summary*   │
│   │
│ ♫ *Syncopation occurs when the music fails to meet our expectation of a strong beat.* │
│   │
│ ♫ *Syncopation typically occurs when a note on a weak part of the measure is made* │
│ *stronger than its surrounding notes: by lengthening it ('giving it 'rhythmic weight') or* │
│ *accenting it (that is, making it louder).* │
│   │
└───┘

ⓘ Supplemental Lesson
Examples from the Repertoire

In this supplemental lesson we'll take a look at a few more examples of syncopation from the music of the great composers. The rhythms are shown with the pulse underneath. This should help you observe how the syncopations don't line up with the typical pattern of strong and weak beats of the meter. It's a good idea to find the full scores of these pieces (at *imslp.org*) and to listen to them as you read the music.

1. Mozart - Symphony no. 25: The introduction of this symphony features a syncopated rhythm in the violins. The syncopation is made even more striking because it takes place on top of a regular pulse in the basses. The effect overall is a dramatic introduction to the whole symphony.

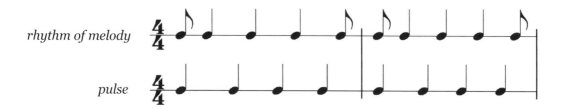

2. Boccherini – Minuet: Here's a similar rhythm as Mozart's but used in three-four for an entirely different effect. Notice the upbeat that sets it up:

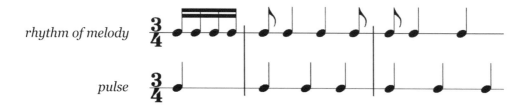

3. Cui Cesar – Op. 64 no. 13: This simple syncopated rhythm is a considerable part of the character of this prelude.

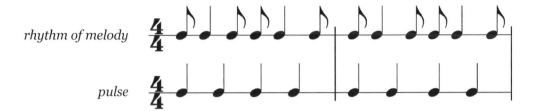

4. Beethoven – 2 Preludes, Op. 39: Since it's so much longer than the surrounding notes, the half note in measure 1 sounds like it's the strong beat and should be at the beginning of the measure. This is what Beethoven wrote:

But since we're at the beginning of the piece, we don't have an established meter to measure the rhythm with and so it sounds more like:

Beethoven sets this up on purpose. Once new notes come in to fill the space that the long note creates, the meter is established clearly.

👁 🎧 Listening & Score Reading Challenge 1

Here are some suggested pieces for listening. When possible also find the score so that you can follow the written music too. This is known as *score reading*.

If you've never done this before, you might get lost in the score a few times. This is normal and you shouldn't worry. Just go back and continue as you can. This is not a test; it's all about the experience.

1. Beethoven: Theme and Variations in F, op. 34

What to listen for: This piece consists of 9 movements (9 parts): a theme and 8 variations. The theme is in simple duple meter, marked *Adagio* but it changes character many times as Beethoven plays around with the meter and tempo in the variations. Listen for these changes of character of the music produced by the changes in tempo and meter.

2. Charles Ives: The Unanswered Question

What to listen for: The sustained chords, played by the strings, create a feeling of timelessness due to the extremely slow tempo.

3. Debussy: Arabesque no. 1

What to listen for: Listen to the characteristic triplets inside a simple quadruple meter and notice the many instructions on the score related to tempo changes (these are dealt with in detail in later lessons).

4. Holst: Mars, from the Planets, op. 32

What to listen for: The rhythmic drive is overt in this piece. Listen for the quintuple meter, five-four, all throughout except for a middle section in five-two meter.

5. Wagner: Tristan und Isolde Prelude

What to listen for: Notice the long rests in between moments of sounds at the beginning of this prelude. The silences are as important as the tones themselves to impart the intended dramatic quality of the music.

Exercises for Day 15

1. Mark the syncopations in these rhythms.

Part 2
The Organization of Pitch

In music, the word *pitch* refers to our perception of how high or low a tone is. Pitch comes to our ears in the form of waves of energy, specifically sound waves. A sound wave pulsates through air, reaches our ears and is then interpreted as sound by our brain. The sound wave is very much like ripples of water or like wind moving a field of grass. Instead of water or grass, sound moves through the air that surrounds us.

There are 2 basic types of sound waves: **uniform** waves and **random** waves. The pitches produced by random waves are **indefinite.** We perceive these sounds as *noise,* or in musical terms *percussive.* Examples include countless everyday things such as ripping paper, a hammer hitting a wall, breaking glass and running water. Drums and many other percussion instruments also produce indefinite pitch.

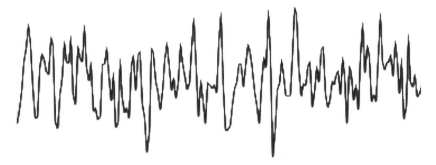

A random wave

The pitches produced by uniform waves, on the other hand, are **definite** and we perceive them as *musical tones*. Examples include singing, humming, and all the tones produced by musical instruments.

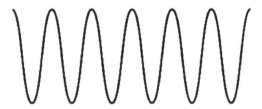

A uniform wave

In our study of pitch of this chapter, we are mainly concerned with definite pitches. We will first learn how these pitches are organized to produce the basis of our musical language (days 16 and 17) and then we will see how to represent these different pitches in musical notation (day 18 to 24).

Day 16
The Musical Alphabet & the Keyboard

Even though this is not a course on piano playing, it's very, very useful to become familiar with the keyboard because it makes the visualization of theoretical concepts much easier. For the rest of this course, it will be quite handy to have a piano or keyboard close by.

> *If you don't have a piano or keyboard at hand, there are many online apps that you can use for free. Simply search for 'virtual keyboard' and many choices will come up.*

Looking at a piano, we should easily notice that there is a particular, recurring pattern to how the keys are organized. The pattern consists of **12 keys: 7 white and 5 black** and it repeats itself several times throughout the entire keyboard. In the diagram below, the pattern occurs 3 times:

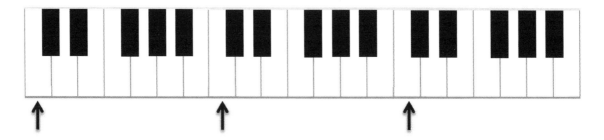

And here is one instance of it, consisting of 12 keys: 7 white and 5 black:

These 12 keys that make up one pattern on the keyboard are the **12 different tones (or pitches) that make up our alphabet of music**. The keys going to the left produce lower and lower pitches while those to the right produce higher and higher pitches.

Naming Notes

The 7 white key notes are named using the first 7 letters of the English alphabet: A, B, C, D, E, F and G. (We will deal with the black keys later).

And as we've seen, the pattern

repeats up and down the keyboard, so after the note *G*, we get another *A* note and the pattern starts over again from *A* to *G*. Here is the keyboard starting from the note *C* and going through all the white keys twice over.

The Octave

Notice that **the distance between two notes that share the same letter name is of 8 keys**, or 8 notes. For example, there are 8 notes from this first *C* note to the next *C* note:

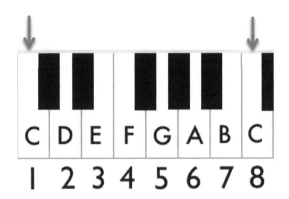

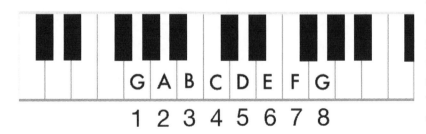

This distance is called **the octave**. The word comes from Latin meaning *'eight'* and in music we use it to refer to the **distance of eight notes**. So from one *G* note to the next *G* note is the distance of an octave.

As well as from one *E* note to the next *E* note:

And so on-the distance between 2 notes that share the same letter name is that of an octave.

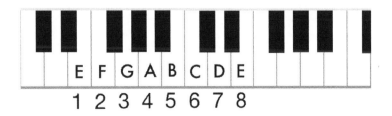

83

Now try it out for yourself. Play and listen to two A notes. Notice how they sound the same except that one is higher (or lighter) and one is lower (or heavier and darker).

When reading about music theory and composition, you will find that the word *octave* is used in different ways. Keep in mind that it always refers to the same thing: a distance of 8 notes.

For example, the C note numbered 8 in the picture below is an **octave higher** than the other C. Or vice-versa: the 1st C note is an **octave lower** than the other C note.

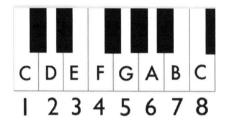

We can also say that these two *F* notes are **an octave apart**. They are 8 notes (or keys) apart.

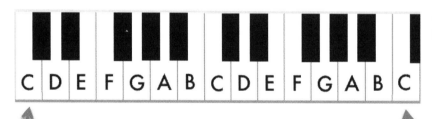

And these two C notes are **two octaves apart**.

When counting distance between musical tones, both the first and the last tone are included in the sum. In the example above, the first 'C' note is counted as 1.

Octave Number

In music we have a vast range of notes spanning approximately 8 octaves and this means that each letter name of the musical alphabet is repeated many times. A standard piano keyboard, for example, has 8 different C notes spread across 88 keys.

In order to distinguish between the notes that share a letter name, the octaves are numbered from zero to nine. This numbering system is called the **Scientific Pitch Notation (SPN)** and it helps us to **refer to a specific note by specifying its octave.** In this system, any one octave begins on a C, goes through D, E, F, G, A and ends on a B.

The first octave, then, are the notes:

$$C0, D0, E0, F0, G0, A0 \text{ and } B0.$$

And the second octave comprises the notes:

$$C1, D1, E1, F1, G1, A1 \text{ and } B1.$$

As we've said, this numbering will be useful when we speak of specific pitches. The lowest note of the piano, for example, is specifically the note A0 (and not just any A note) while the highest is C8 (and not just any C note). Another example is that the four strings of the violin are tuned specifically at G3, D4, A4 and E5.

Day 16 Quick Summary

♫ *There are 12 notes in the musical alphabet.*

♫ *The 12 notes are laid out as 7 white keys and 5 black keys on the piano.*

♫ *The white keys are named A, B, C, D, E, F and G.*

♫ *The distance between two notes that share the same letter name is of 8 notes and it's known as the octave.*

Exercises for Day 16

1. Fill in the blanks.

        a. The musical alphabet consists of _____ keys.

        b. _____ are white keys.

        c. And _____ are black.

2. Fill in the blanks.

        a. The white keys are named using which letters of the English alphabet?

        _____

        b. The distance between two keys that share the same letter-names is of _____ keys. This distance is known as 'an _____'.

        c. Mark this distance on this keyboard diagram.

3. Since the musical alphabet repeats itself many times, we make use of SPN.

        a. What does SPN stand for? _____

        b. SPN is helpful because it allows us to refer to a specific note by

        _____.

Day 17
Musical Steps

The Half Step

In the previous lesson you might have noticed that within one octave on the piano, there are two pairs of keys that do not have a black key between them.

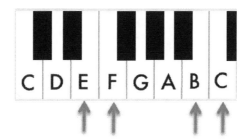

This means that these notes are the **smallest distance possible** between any two notes. This distance is known as a **half step**.

A half step on the keyboard is **the distance from any one key to the key immediately next to it.** Whether this distance is to the right or the left of the keyboard, and whether the keys are black or white doesn't matter – if they are immediately next to each other, they are a half step.

So if we play an *E* and want to ascend a half step (which means going up to the nearest note), we get an *F*. And similarly, if we play the note *C* and want to descend a half step (going down to the next note), we get the note *B*.

If we start from an *F* note and ascend a half step, we get to the black key above it (the names of the black keys are discussed fully in the next lesson):

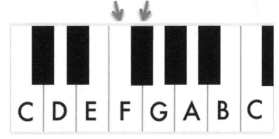

And if we start from a *D* note and descend a half step, we get to the black key below it.

The Whole Step

A whole step is the distance of two half steps. It's **the distance between any two keys that have one intervening key in between.**

To ascend a whole step from D, for example, we simply skip a note and we end up on E.

Now let's descend a whole step down from G. One half step down takes us to the black note to its left, and one more half step takes down to F. So the distance between F and G is of a whole step.

So within the musical alphabet we've learned thus far, there are 2 half steps and 5 whole steps. As we've seen, the half steps are between the notes *E* and *F* and the notes *B* and *C*. Keeping in mind that **1 whole step equals 2 half steps**, the whole steps are:

From *C* to *D*:

D to *E*:

F to *G*:

G to *A*:

88

And *A* to *B*:

Just like the half step, the distance of the whole step applies exactly the same way to the black keys as well. For example, a whole step up from the note *E* is the next black key.

While a whole step down from *C* is this black key:

And of course, there can be whole steps between black keys only. In this example on the left, the whole step is between 2 black keys, specifically the ones that are separated by the note *G*.

Half steps and whole steps are important because they are our first way of measuring distances between notes. In book 2 of this series, you will learn all the distances between any two keys.

Day 17 Quick Summary

♫ *The half step is the distance between any one note to the note immediately next to it. It's the shortest possible distance between any two keys on the keyboard.*

♫ *The whole step is equal to 2 half steps. It's the distance between any two keys that have one intervening key in between.*

Exercises for Day 17

1. Mark the key that is a half step **below** the indicated note:

a.

b.

c.

d.

2. Mark the key that is a half step **above** the indicated note:

a.

b.

c.

d.

3. Mark the key that is a whole step below the indicated note:

a.

b.

c.

d.

4. Mark the key that is a whole step above the indicated note:

a.

b.

c.

d.

5. On a keyboard (real or online) play and sing any whole step. Then play and sing any half step. Compare these sounds; listen closely to the difference between the half step and the whole step. It might be subtle at first but it's definitely there!

Now that your ear is warmed up go to _www.schoolofcomposition.com/extras_ to access the audio for the listening challenge below.

👂 Listening Challenge: **Is it a Whole Step or a Half Step?**

In this listening challenge you'll find 12 pairs of notes. Your task is to determine which notes are a whole step apart and which are a half step apart just by listening.

Write W for whole step and H for half step:

1. _____   6. _____
2. _____   7. _____
3. _____   8. _____
4. _____   9. _____
5. _____   10. _____

Day 18
Accidentals

So far we learned what the notes of the white keys on the piano are called. We learned that there is a pattern of 7 letter names given to 7 pitches and they go from *A* all the way up to *G*. (Or in the other direction, from *G* all the way down to *A*).

The black keys, of course, are the other 5 notes (out of the 12) of our musical alphabet. These five new notes are also named using the alphabet from *A* to *G*, but in order to distinguish the differences between them and the white keys, we add **accidentals.**

There are three basic accidentals and their function is **to raise or lower a note by one half step.** Let's look at the first two accidentals and their symbols that are used in musical notation: the sharp and the flat.

The Sharp

The sharp is written like this:

And its job is to raise the pitch of a note by a half step. This means that putting a sharp next to a note, gives us the note that is immediately above it. This new note will have **two parts to its name: the letter name of the original note and the word *sharp*.**

For example, putting a sharp next to the note *C* will give us the note *C sharp* (or we could write it as 'C#') and its sound will be a half step higher then the note *C*.

Similarly, *G sharp* is a half step higher than *G*.

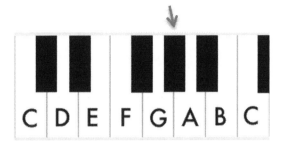

And so on and so forth, the names of the remaining black keys are as follows:

D sharp:

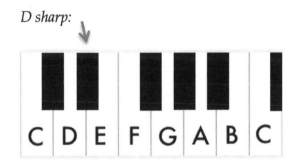

F sharp:

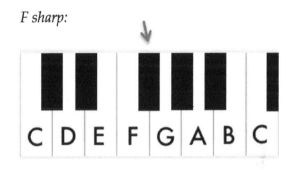

And *A sharp*:

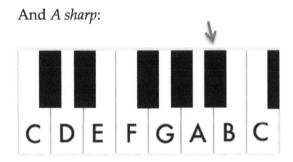

With the addition of sharpened notes our musical alphabet now consists of 12 different notes:

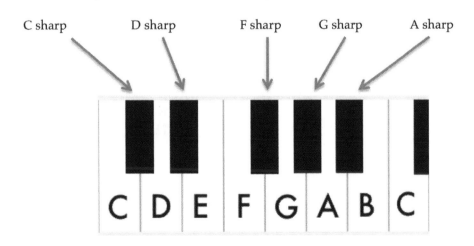

The Flat

The second type of accidental is called **the Flat** and this is its symbol:

While **the sharp raises the pitch by a half step, the flat lowers it by a half step**. This means that putting a flat next to a note, gives us the note that is immediately below it. Just like before, these new notes will have **two parts to their name: the letter name of the original note and the word** *flat.*

For example, putting a flat next to the note *B* will give us the note *B flat* (or we could write it like: *Bb*) and its sound will be lower than B by a half step.

This key is *E flat*. It sounds a half step lower than the note *E*.

Similarly, this is *A flat:*   *G flat:*

And *D flat:*

At this point you might be wondering why we are renaming the black keys with flats once we've already learned their names with sharps. This is because the 5 notes that are the black keys on the piano have two alternate names – one with a sharp and one with a flat. This concept is called **enharmonic equivalence** and it's explained fully in the next pages.

Our 12 tone musical alphabet is now complete. We have our usual 7 white keys named after the first 7 letters of the English alphabet and 5 black keys, each one with 2 possible names:

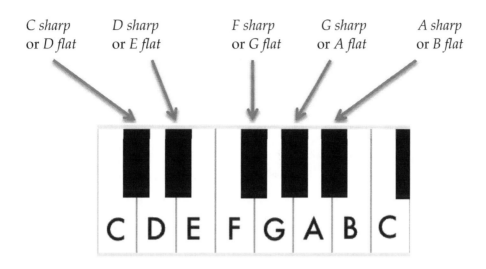

Enharmonic Equivalence

Enharmonic equivalence is the fancy term for having **two different names** (or two different spellings) **for one sound** (one musical note).

The reason that some notes have 2 alternate names is because of how the concept of the sharp and flat works. The **sharp raises *any* note** by a half step while the flat **lowers *any* note** by a half step no matter what the original note being altered is. So the note that is a half step higher than *D*, for example, is a *D sharp*. But at the same time, that same note is a half step lower than *E* so its name could also be *E flat*.

It's a common misconception that only the white keys can be sharpened or flattened and that only the black keys are named as sharps or flats. In reality, any note can be raised or lowered: whether it is a *B*, an *F*, an *E*, a *G*, etc. or even, as we shall see, an *E flat*, a *C sharp* or any other black key.

For example, sharpening the note *E* will give us the note *E sharp*. And, of course, this is an enharmonic equivalent of the note *F*. This means that *F* and *E sharp* are two names for the same sound. The question of which name to use for the note depends on context. This is a more advanced issue and so we don't need to worry about it here.

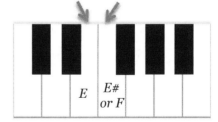

The Natural

What happens if we need to raise a flattened note? Or lower a sharpened note? <u>How does an altered note go back to the original, unaltered note?</u>

This is where the third accidental becomes useful. Its name is **the natural** and it is written like this:

Its job is to **cancel a sharp or a flat** that has appeared before. For example, if we need to write the notes C *sharp* and then C, we make our intentions clear that the second note is not sharpened (that it is not another C *sharp*), by using the natural. As we shall see, without this accidental, a note could easily be misinterpreted.

The natural is also used to cancel out a flat. For example, if we need to write the note E *flat* followed by the note above it, E, we use the natural to make it clear that this second E is not flattened too.

The natural, therefore, has the power to both raise and lower notes. **When it cancels a sharp, it lowers the note by a half step** and therefore takes it back to the original. **When it cancels a flat, it raises the note by a half step** and takes it back to the original.

The Double Accidentals

We mentioned earlier that **flattened notes could be flattened further, and sharpened notes sharpened further.** This is where the **double sharp** and the **double flat** come in. These accidentals are not as common as the other three but they are good to know anyway.

The Double Sharp

The symbol for the double sharp is this:

And its job is to **raise the note by a whole step**. For example, double sharpening the note F produces the note F *double sharp*.

The F *double sharp*, of course, is an enharmonic equivalent of the note G.

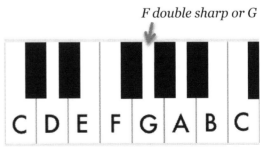

F double sharp or G

The Double Flat

The symbol for the double flat is this:

And its job is to **lower the note by a whole step**. For example, double flattening the note *E* produces the note *E double flat* and it is an enharmonic equivalent of the note *D*.

E double flat or D:

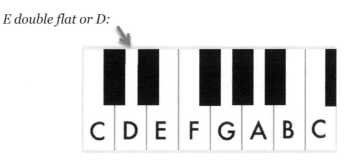

Due to all these accidentals, any note out of the 12 can have at least one alternate name – that is, an enharmonic equivalent.

Notation

Accidentals are written on the left of the note, in line with the note head and they remain in effect for the whole measure.

Day 18 Quick Summary

♫ *The sharp raises the note by a half step.*

♫ *The flat lowers the note by a half step.*

♫ *The natural cancels sharps or flats.*

♫ *The double sharp raises the note by a whole step.*

♫ *The double flat lowers the note by a whole step.*

Exercises for Day 18

1a. Which one of these accidentals is the sharp?

b. Its function is to _____ the note by a half step.

2a. Which one of these accidentals is the flat?

b. Its function is to _____ the note by a half step.

3a. Which one of these accidentals is the natural?

Its function is to _____ .

4. Use the diagrams below to mark the indicated notes.

     a. *F sharp*   b. *E flat*

c. G natural

d. D double sharp

e. A sharp

f. B double flat

g. G flat

h. F flat

5. What is an enharmonic equivalent of:

a. *D* sharp = <u>*E flat*</u>

b. *F* flat = _____

c. *B* sharp = _____

d. *G* sharp = _____

e. *A sharp* = _____

f. *A double sharp* = _____

g. *C natural* = _____

h. *G double sharp* = _____

Day 19
Notating Pitch: The Staff

Since we perceive musical tones as higher or lower in relation to each other, we need a system of notation that can visually represent these relations. **The staff – a set of 5 parallel, horizontal lines**, provides such a system.

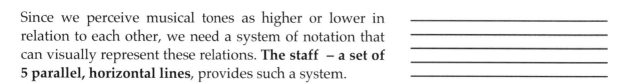

> *It's interesting to note that another word for staff is 'stave' but the word 'staves' is plural to both 'staff' and 'stave'.*

Musical notes will be written out through the 5 lines:

As well as in the 4 spaces between the lines:

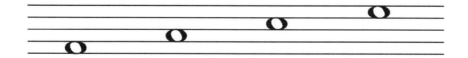

Notes that sound higher are placed higher on the staff and notes that sound lower are placed lower. Keeping in mind that notes on the staff are read from left to right (→), just like written English, we can see that notes can move in 3 ways:

1. Up or down to the next space or line, known in musical terms as **stepwise motion**:

2. Up or down by more than a step, known as **skipwise motion**:

3. Or the same note can be played again (repeated), known as **stationary motion:**

Tones that are sounded together are written on top of each other like so:

Exercises for Day 19

1. How many lines make up the musical staff? _____

2. On this empty staff, write: a) two different notes that go **through a line**, and b) two different notes that are **in the spaces between the lines**.

3. On this empty staff, write a pair of notes that move a) in stepwise motion and b) in skipwise motion:

Day 20
Ledger Lines: Beyond the Staff

Although the 5 lines and 4 spaces of the staff are already quite efficient at representing tones visually, we do also have a means of representing higher or lower notes than the staff would normally allow.

We do so simply by adding lines, as they are needed, either on top of the staff for notes that go higher:

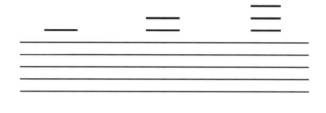

Or below, for notes that go lower:

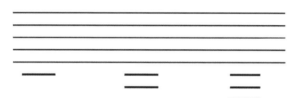

These extra lines are called **ledger lines** (also spelled *Leger*). Just like on the normal staff, notes can be placed through the ledger lines themselves:

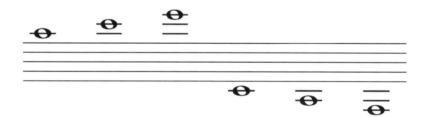

Or in between the spaces:

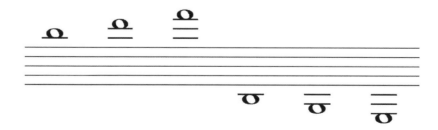

*A warning: notation is meant to provide the reader with an **easily and quickly discernible** musical score (sheet music). Having too many ledger lines makes it difficult to recognize what the notes are so ledger lines are usually limited to about 4 or 5.*

Accidentals that belong to notes on ledger lines are no different than normal. They are written to the left of the note and parallel to the note head:

Exercises for Day 20

1. To go higher or lower than the staff would normally allow, we employ _____ lines.

2. Write three to five notes with high ledger lines on this empty staff:

3. Write three to five notes with low ledger lines on this empty staff:

4. Write three to five notes that **do not** employ any ledger lines:

Day 21
The Treble Clef

So how can the staff of only 5 lines and 4 spaces be used to represent all the notes that we can hear in music? Whether we listen to classical, rock, pop, jazz, hip-hop, etc. there are pitches that are very high and other pitches that are very low. How do the staff and a few ledger lines manage all that?

The answer is in the **clef**.

The clef (from Latin, *clavis* meaning a key) is a symbol that tells us **which ranges of notes are going to be represented on that particular staff.** There have been numerous clefs that were used throughout the history of music but the most common nowadays are two: the **bass clef** for low notes and the **treble clef** for higher notes.

Without a clef, we wouldn't be able to identify which note is which.

And because of this, **the clef is the first symbol to be placed on the staff**.

The Treble Clef

The clef that is most used in our times is the treble clef:

If you've never drawn a treble clef, try it in steps:

1. Start with this curl, going clockwise.

2. Continue upwards as if writing a number six.

3. Prepare the twist in the opposite direction.

4. Draw the line going down.

5. And finish it off with an inward twirl.

The treble clef is used for notes that are relatively high. Originally it was part of a group of clefs known as the **G clefs**. They were called so because their job was to **designate where the note G is** on the staff and this depended on where exactly the clef was drawn.

For example, if the G clef was drawn starting from the first (the lowest) line:

Then the note on that line itself becomes the note G (specifically G4 in SPN). Once we've determined where G is, we can work out what the other notes are, by counting up and down the musical alphabet.

The G clef that we are familiar with today is the **Treble Clef** and it indicates that **the note G is on the 2nd line of the staff**.

And so the notes on the treble clef are:

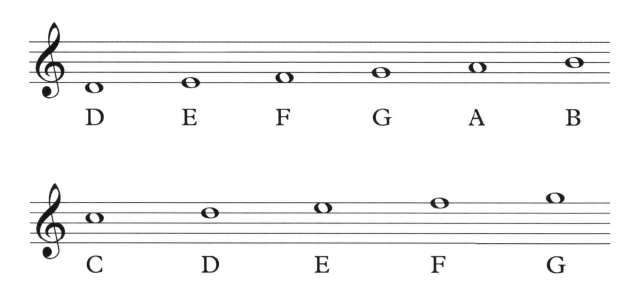

ⓘ Expert Tip: **Reading the Treble Clef Quickly**

Here are two common tricks to help you figure out the notes on the treble clef quicker. The first four spaces spell out the word: FACE

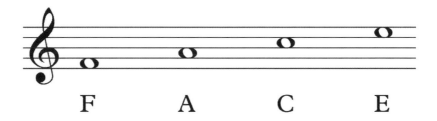

And the notes on the lines are E - G - B - D - F – which are an acronym of *'Every Good Boy Deserves Fun'*:

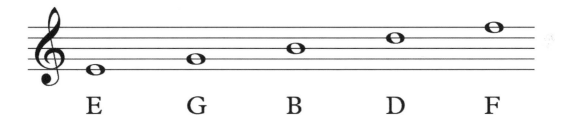

Apart from that always keep in mind that the middle line is a *B* and you can count backwards or upwards through the alphabet. The note below *B* is an *A*, and the one above it is a *C* and so on.

Here is an example of a tune on the treble clef, originally for violin. Can you name all the notes? *(Notice the use of a ledger line above the staff and that it begins on an upbeat).*

Audio Example 21.1: Bach - Violin Concerto BWV 1041

Exercises for Day 21

1. Name these notes on the treble clef:

2. On the empty staff below, draw a treble clef and then write these notes *(in whichever octave you prefer)*:

    a. *B flat*   b. *G*   c. *B natural*
    d. *C sharp*   e. *A flat*   f. *D*
    g. *F*   h. *F sharp*   i. *E flat*

Day 22
All About that Bass Clef

While the treble clef is used to represent relatively high pitches, the bass clef is used to represent lower pitches. The bass clef is written like this (the two dots are important too):

Originally the Bass clef was part of a group of clefs known as the **'F clefs'**. Just like the G clefs, the F clefs would be drawn higher or lower on the staff depending on what was necessary. The two dots of the symbol would indicate where the note 'F' is *(specifically F3)*. Of course, once we determine where the note 'F' is, we can work out what the other notes are by counting up and down our musical alphabet.

The Bass clef we use today is the *F* clef written in such a way to mark the note *F* on the 4th line of the staff.

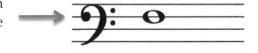

And the notes on the bass clef then become named so:

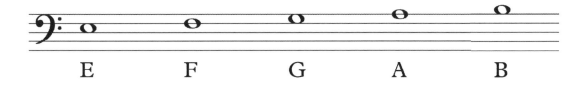

F   G   A   B   C   D

E   F   G   A   B

The tips for reading the treble clef quicker apply just the same for the bass clef. These notes spell the word FACE:

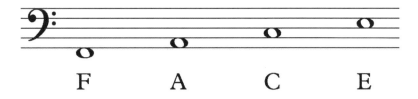

F   A   C   E

And the notes on the lines spell out - G – B – D – F – A - which you might remember with the phrase '*Good Boys Deserve Fun Always*':

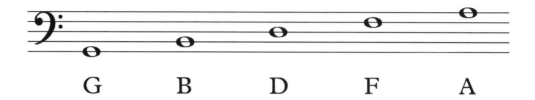

Here is an example of a tune on the bass clef, originally for cello. Can you name all the notes?

pp

Audio Example 22.1: Schubert - Symphony No. 8, 1st movement

The Grand Staff

Since it has so many keys (88 to be exact) the piano uses two staves. The bottom one for the Bass clef, played by the left hand, and the top one for the treble, played by the right hand. In music notation, the staves will be joined by a brace and so it becomes what is known as **the grand staff** (or *the great staff*).

Brace

Beethoven: Piano Sonata No. 3

Other instruments that use the grand staff include other keyboards (such as the organ, celesta and accordion) as well as the harp.

Exercises for Day 22

1. Name these notes.

2. On the empty staff below, draw a bass clef and then write these notes *(in whichever octave you prefer)*:

a. *B flat*   b. *G*   c. *B natural*
d. *C sharp*   e. *A flat*   f. *D*
g, *E*   h. *F sharp*   i. *A*

Day 23
The C Clefs: Alto & Tenor

Since we're now familiar with the two most common clefs, we'll now examine the *C Clefs.* These are also still in use today but not as widespread as the treble and the bass clefs.

 The C clef is this symbol on the left and, as the name suggests, it indicates where the note C is (specifically *C4,* also known as the *Middle C*). When the C clef is placed in such a way that shows the middle line to be the note C, it becomes the **Alto Clef**. Instruments that use this clef include the viola and the trombone.

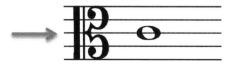

Of course, once any one note is established on the staff, we can know the other notes by counting up and down the musical alphabet.

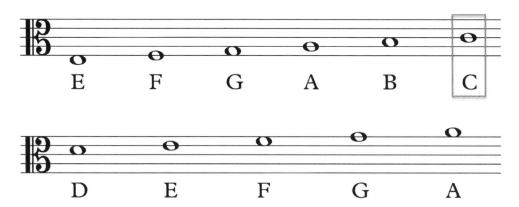

When the C clef is placed in such a way that shows the fourth line to be the note C, it becomes the **Tenor Clef**. This clef is used mostly for the higher ranges of the Bassoon, Trombone and Cello.

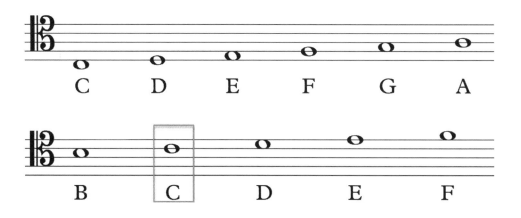

Exercises for Day 23

1. Name these notes on the alto clef:

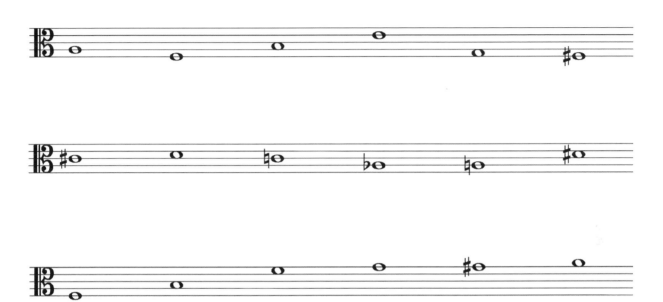

2. Name these notes on the tenor clef:

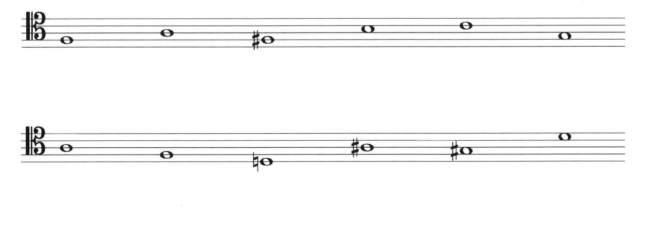

Day 24
One Stem to Rule Them All (& Other Issues)

The Note Stem Rule

The note stem rule concerns the direction of the stem of a note. In order to write music neatly, the rule states that: If the **note head is on or above the middle line of the staff, the stem points down** - If the **note head is below the middle line, the stem points up:**

This rule should help make written music easier to read because, as the examples on this page show, most stems will stay within the staff. Perhaps more importantly is that notes on the grand staff don't collide into each other:

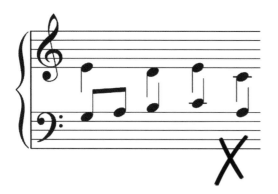

The rule, however, is ignored if it means that the music will be neater and clearer. In the example below, the last two eighth notes (a *B* and a *C*) have stems going up but this is because they are part of a larger group of beamed notes. *I'm sure we can agree that these 6 notes are neat and clear, so they're fine!*

Multiple Voices on a Staff

The note stem rule is neglected also when one staff serves for writing 2 separate voices or parts. The word *'voices'* here refers to **distinct, individual musical lines** and it doesn't necessarily mean that they are sung. Neither does it necessarily mean that two different instruments play the two lines although this is possible too. In this example by Bach, one guitar plays the 2 distinct and separate lines (2 voices).

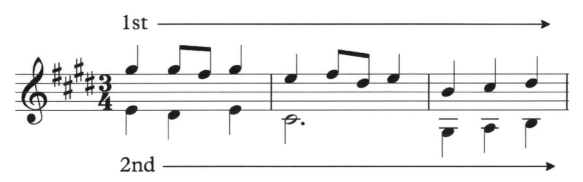

Bach: Minuet 1 from Lute Suite no. 4, BWV 1006a

Notice how all the stems of the 1st voice point upwards and those of the 2nd voice point downwards. This is done so that the voices remain clearly distinct at all time. The alternative, conforming to the note stem rule, is barely legible:

Writing Rests on the Staff

Finally, take note of how the rests are written on the staff. As the diagram below shows, the whole rest hangs on the fourth line, the half rest sits on the third line and the others are written around the middle of the staff.

Whole rest	Half rest	Quarter Rest	Eighth Rest	Sixteenth Rest

Exercises for Day 24

1. Change these whole notes into half notes by adding a stem. *Make sure of the correct stem direction.*

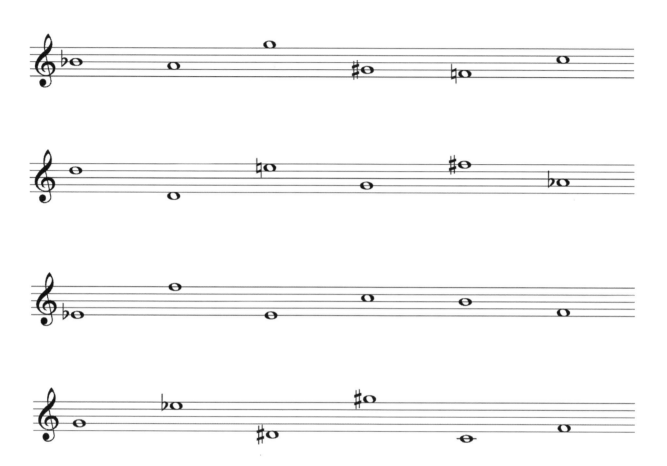

2. Indicate with a circle which of these stems are in the wrong direction:

👁 🎶 Listening & Score Reading Challenge 2

For this challenge your task is to read the sheet music *(available at imslp.org)* while listening to a recording of these compositions *(all available on YouTube at the time of this writing)*. Suggestions for what to listen for are listed with every piece below.

1. Beethoven: Symphony no. 9, op. 125, 4th movement

What to listen for: Note how this popular theme consists mostly of whole steps and half steps. Throughout the music, the theme is developed, varied and transformed in various ways but its characteristic stepwise movement is consistent.

2. De Victoria: Taedet Animam Meam

What to listen for: This piece is from the 16th Century. Notice the musical effects produced by the added sharps and flats. At that time this was a relatively new style of music.

3. Grieg: Holberg Suite (String Orchestra Version)

What to listen for: This piece was originally for piano and the composer himself arranged it for string orchestra. Observe the interactions between the four instruments (first violins, second violins, violas and cellos) and notice the 3 clefs in use: the violins are in the treble clef, the violas in the alto clef and the cellos in the bass clef. Together they cover a very wide range of notes.

4. Bach: Bourrée in E minor from Lute Suite No. 1, BWV 996

What to listen for: Although it was originally for Lute, this piece has become a timeless standard for the Classical Guitar. It is known for Bach's masterful use of 2 voices at the same time (a compositional technique known as counterpoint). Notice how the 2 voices share one staff: the top voice has stems going up and the bottom voice has stems going down. This way the music is clear to read.

5. Schubert – Fantasia for Piano 4 Hands, D. 940

What to listen for: As its title says, this piece is for 2 players (4 hands) on 1 piano. The music is written on 2 grand staffs, one for each pianist. The first pianist takes up the top two parts and the second takes the lower two parts. The interaction between the two is fascinating!

Part 3
Giving Life to your Notes with Musical Expression

Apart from rhythm and pitch, composers add several other marks, symbols and instructions to their written music so that their intentions for what it should sound like are as clear as possible.

By the end of this chapter, you will be able to recognize what the markings on this score, and many others, mean.

Audio Example 25.1: Beethoven: Piano Sonata no.32, 1st movement, measures 1, 2

This is the last section of the book and it consists of five lessons:

Day 25: Dynamics – how loud or soft a note should be played;

Day 26: Articulation – instructions for how notes should sound;

Day 27: Tempo – a variety of effects on the pace of the music (such as slowing down);

Day 28: Bar lines and repeat signs;

Day 29: Expression marks specific to the piano.

Day 25
Dynamics

Dynamics are symbols that indicate how loud or soft a note should be played.

The specific term for **loud** is the Italian word *forte* and the symbol is this:

The term for **soft** (or quiet) is *piano* and the symbol is this:

f

p

Dynamic markings are written just below the note. Notice the *forte* and *piano* signs here:

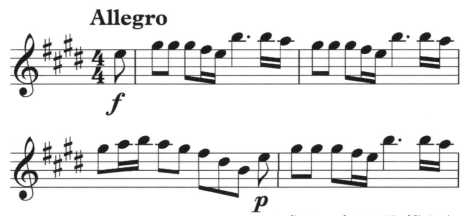

Audio Example 25.2: Vivaldi: Spring, 1st movement

In addition to these two, we have symbols that indicate more specific nuances of loudness or softness. As you can see in the table here, adding more *piano* signs indicates softer dynamics while adding more *forte* signs indicates louder dynamics.

In between these two poles of loud and soft, we have two moderate dynamics: *Mezzo piano* meaning **moderately soft** and *mezzo forte* meaning **moderately loud**.

Musical Term	Meaning	Symbol
pianississimo	very, very soft	ppp
pianissimo	very soft	pp
piano	soft	p
mezzo piano	moderately soft	mp
mezzo forte	moderately loud	mf
forte	loud	f
fortissimo	very loud	ff
fortississimo	very, very loud	fff

119

Allegretto frescamente ♩ = 80

Audio Example 25.3: Medtner: 4 Tales, Op. 26, Allegretto frescamente

Even more extreme dynamics are sometimes called for and these are written simply by adding more $\boldsymbol{p}$ for more softness and more $\boldsymbol{f}$ for more loudness. Keep in mind that these dynamics are not specific measurements of loudness and softness. A great deal depends on context such as instrumentation and range.

---

*Dynamics are not just about volume. When an instrument is played loudly or softly, its sound quality changes. Think about it this way: if we record a flute playing forte and then play that recording back at a low volume, the music doesn't become 'piano'. The **sound quality** of the instrument is still of a* **forte** *– it's just played back at a lower volume.*

Gradual Changes

Apart from *piano* and *forte*, we also have symbols to instruct the performer that the music **becomes louder or softer little by little**. The musical term for **gradually getting louder** is the Italian word *crescendo*.

Audio Example 25.4: Clementi: Sonatina No.1, Op. 46, measures 28 – 31

It is often shortened simply as *cresc.* (such as in example 25.4) or replaced entirely by this symbol known as a hairpin:

Gradually getting **louder & louder**

Audio Example 25.5: Rachmaninov: Prelude in G minor, Op. 23 No. 5

The term for gradually getting softer is the Italian word **diminuendo,** often simply shortened to **dim.**

Audio Example 25.6 Handel: Largo from Xerxes, measures 7 - 10

The word *dim.* can also be replaced by the hairpin going in the opposite direction:

Gradually getting softer & softer

Audio Example 25.7: Poulenc: Suite pour Piano, FP 19

Another word for *diminuendo* is *decrescendo* and it abbreviated as *decresc.*

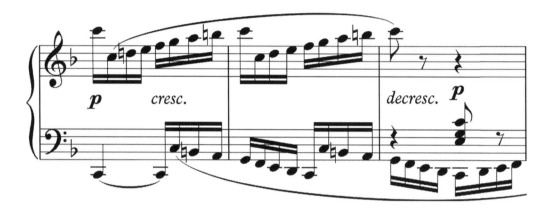

Audio Example 25.8: Beethoven: Piano Sonata No. 22, 2ⁿᵈ movement, measures 16 - 18

The word *crescendo* is sometimes stretched out over several measures so that its execution is prolonged. Notice how the dashed line connects the various parts of the word.

Audio Example 25.9: Reger: Cello Suite no. 1 in G major, Op. 131c, Prelude

The words **poco** (Italian for **a little**) and **molto** (Italian for **a lot**) can be added to *crescendos* and *diminuendos* to specify better the degree of change. In the following example we have '***poco cresc***' meaning '***getting a little louder***' and then '***cresc molto***' meaning '***getting a lot louder.***'

122

Audio Example 25.10 Bartok: Bagatelle No. 4, Op. 6, measures 6 - 9

Sudden Changes

Dynamic changes are not always gradual. Composers often call for sudden and abrupt changes as well. One of the simplest ways of notating an abrupt dynamic change is to add the word *subito* (shortened simply as *sub.*) to the standard dynamic symbols. *Subito* is Italian for *sudden*. In this example we have a *'subito piano'* meaning *'suddenly soft'*

.

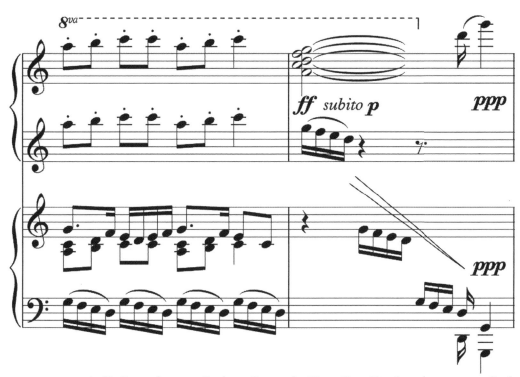

Audio Example 25.11: Poulenc: Sonata for Piano Four Hands, 2nd movement, final measures

When a note or a group of notes are to be played loudly followed immediately by softer notes, we have the indication *forte piano* (meaning *'loud and then immediately soft'*).

The symbol is this: **fp**

123

Audio Example 25.12: Mozart: Fantasia no. 4 in C minor, K. 475, measures 7 - 9

To emphasize a specific note (or notes), we have the marking **sforzando**, shortened simply as **sfz**. *Sforzando* is the Italian word for *forcing* or *with force*. In music it suggests a sudden emphasis.

Audio Example 25.13: Mendelssohn: Songs Without Words, Op. 19, No. 6

The terms *sforzato* and *forzato* (or *forzando*) are common alternatives to the word *sforzando* and its abbreviation. They all indicate the same effect.

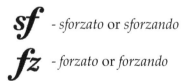

sf - *sforzato* or *sforzando*

fz - *forzato* or *forzando*

Summary of Dynamics

Musical Term	Meaning	Symbol
pianississimo	Very, very soft	*ppp*
pianissimo	Very soft	*pp*
piano	Soft	*p*
mezzo piano	Moderately soft	*mp*
mezzo forte	Moderately loud	*mf*
forte	Loud	*f*
fortissimo	Very loud	*ff*
fortississimo	Very, very loud	*fff*

Gradual Changes	Meaning	Symbol
Crescendo	Gradually getting louder	
Diminuendo	Gradually getting softer	

Sudden Changes	Meaning	Symbol
Forte piano	Loud & then immediately soft	*fp*
Sforzando	Sudden emphasis	*sfz*

Exercises for Day 25

1. Which is the **loudest** dynamic out of these four?

$$\textit{ff} \quad \textit{mp} \quad \textit{pp} \quad \textit{f}$$

2. Which is the **softest** dynamic out of these four?

$$\textit{mf} \quad \textit{p} \quad \textit{fff} \quad \textit{f}$$

3. Which one of these signs means **moderately loud**?

$$\textit{p} \quad \textit{mf} \quad \textit{f} \quad \textit{mp}$$

4. What does this sign mean: ＿＿＿＿＿＿＿＿＿

＿＿＿＿＿＿＿＿＿＿＿＿＿＿＿＿＿＿＿＿

5. What does *diminuendo* mean? ＿＿＿＿＿＿＿＿＿＿＿＿＿

6. What is the symbol for *forte piano*? ＿＿＿＿＿＿＿＿＿＿＿

7. What does this symbol mean? **sfz**

＿＿＿＿＿＿＿＿＿＿＿＿＿＿

👂 Listening Challenge: **What Dynamics?**

In this listening challenge, you have 4 musical extracts with missing dynamic marks. Your task is to listen to the audio and put in all the dynamics details that you can hear. The examples are adaptations from the author's own music.

All clips are downloadable at www.schoolofcomposition.com/extras

1.

Audio Example 25.14

2.

Audio Example 25.15

3.

Audio Example 25.16

4.

Audio Example 25.14

127

Day 26
Articulation

Musicians are able to make notes sound in a variety of ways. Apart from loud and soft, notes can be played smoothly, detached, slightly accented, very accented and so on. In other words, musicians can **articulate** notes in different ways.

Articulation refers to the musician's specific technique when playing a note. But rather than writing instructions for how to breathe, press a key or bow a string for every different instrument, we add **articulation marks** to the notes. These marks indicate how the notes should sound. The exact technical execution is then left up to the musician.

> *This is not to say that technical details are not included in the score. On the contrary, sometimes they are necessary. However, the study of instrumental technique is a vast (and separate) topic so in this chapter we will instead delve into the general aural characteristics of the common articulations and how to notate them in sheet music.*

Legato

Legato means that the notes should be played **as smoothly and as connected as possible**. The idea is that there shouldn't be a gap between the notes. For wind instruments (and voice), legato is achieved by singing two or more notes in one breath – the constant stream of air ensures that the sound is continuous from one note to the next. For bowed string instruments such as the violin, the notes are played in a single, continuous bow movement.

> *To experience legato for yourself, sing, hum or whistle any two different notes in one breath.*

Legato is indicated in written music with a **slur** – a line strung between note heads:

The slur can also be strung over several notes. These 4 notes are played legato:

Andante con moto

Audio Example 26.1: Vieuxtemps: Violin Concerto No. 6, 2ⁿᵈ movement: Pastorale

ⓘ**Expert Tip:** The difference between the tie and the legato slur

This question comes up because the tie and the legato slur are practically the same symbol. To know whether the symbol is a tie or a legato sign is quite simple: ties occur between the **same note at the same octave** (same exact pitch) while the legato slur occurs between two or more different notes.

Staccato

Staccato means that the notes are not connected but **detached** from each other. The musician achieves this effect by shortening the note, usually by about half its original duration.

> *To experience staccato for yourself, sing or whistle any two notes in two different breaths. The different breaths will create a slight gap between the notes.*

The symbol for staccato is a **dot with the note head**. Similar to the legato slur, the staccato dot is written just close to the note head, no matter where the stem points.

129

Audio Example 26.2: Prokofiev: Peter and the Wolf, Theme of the Cat

Staccatissimo

The word *staccattissimo* is the Italian superlative of staccato, meaning that the notes will be **detached and shortened even more** than normal staccato. The symbol for staccattissimo is this:

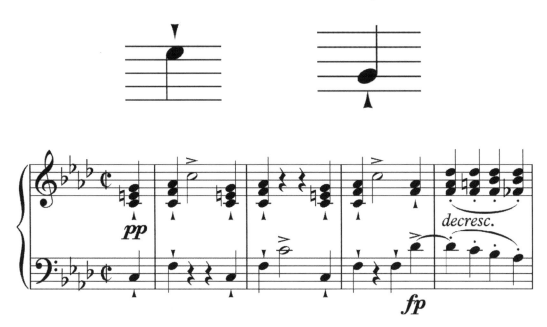

Audio Example 26.3: Schubert: Winterreise, Op. 89, III 'Gefrorne Tränen'

Marcato

The word *marcato* is Italian for **marked**. In music it indicates that a note is **accented** so that it's louder than the surrounding notes.

The exact amount of emphasis a note is given depends a lot on the particular context and the performer's musical decisions. However, we do have two typical kinds of *marcato* signs for varying levels of emphasis.

The standard marcato is usually referred to simply as the **accent** and it's notated as a vertical wedge close to the note head.

130

Audio Example 26.4: Scriabin: Sonata No. 1 in F minor, Op. 6, 1ˢᵗ movement

The other is a horizontal wedge and it is known as **marcato** itself, or **martellato** – Italian for *hammered*. This sign indicates a **stronger** emphasis than the other accent sign.

The *marcato* sign stays on top of the notes, no matter the direction of the stem.

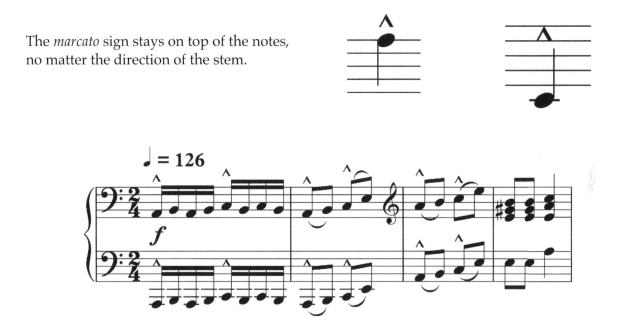

Audio Example 26.5: Schumann: Album for the Young, Op. 68, Knight Rupert

Tenuto

Probably owing to its long history of usage, the *tenuto* mark is one of the least straightforward articulation marks in our entire system of musical notation. The word *tenuto* itself is Italian for *held* and because of this it's often defined as an instruction to *hold the note for all its duration (and nothing less)*. But its actual use by composers reveals that its interpretation depends on its context.

131

The most common interpretations of the tenuto mark are two: firstly **to give the note a slight accent** and secondly, **to extend the note's duration a bit more than its full written value**.

In other words, the tenuto mark indicates an **emphasis**: either through a mild dynamic accent or through a little rhythmic prolongation.

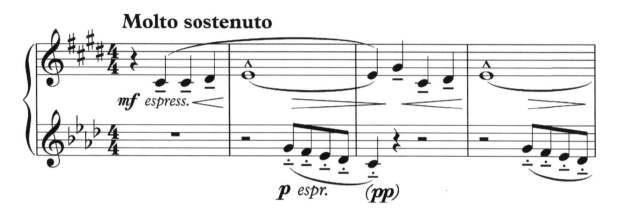

Audio Example 26.6: Bartok: Bagatalle No. 1, Op. 6

An alternative to the tenuto marking is the word *tenuto* itself, usually abbreviated as *ten.*

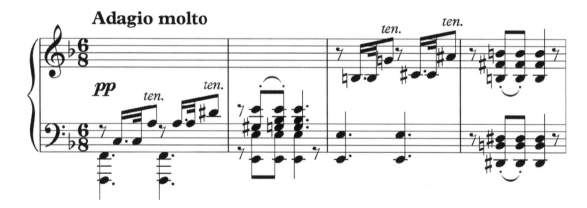

Audio Example 26.7: Beethoven: Piano Sonata No. 21 'Waldstein', 2ⁿᵈ movement, measures 1 - 4

Portato

Portato, also known as **non-legato**, is an interesting articulation in that it is somewhere in between *staccato* and *legato*. In portato, notes are connected and played smoothly (like in *legato*) but they are also individually slightly pronounced. The effect is that the music moves along smoothly with a kind of gentle pulsation to each note.

To experience portato for yourself, sing a group of 3 to 5 notes in one breath (just like legato) and make sure that each note is also gently accentuated (a little like staccato).

The notation for portato combines the staccato dot with the legato slur:

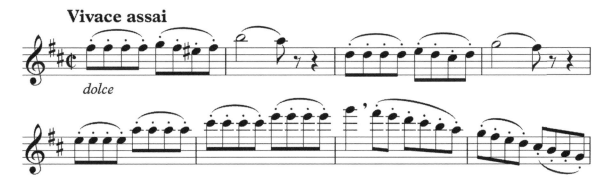

Audio Example 26.8: Drouet: Study No.16 from 72 Studies for the Boehm Flute

Glissando

Glissando is a **slide** from one note to another. When playing any two notes, the instrumentalist would normally move from one to the next avoiding getting any sound from any of the notes in-between. But in glissando those in-between notes are heard as passing through. The effect is a continuous run of adjacent pitches.

The symbol for the glissando is a line with the abbreviation *gliss.* on it. It can go in either direction, up or down:

The glissando effect is synonymous with the harp as it's just natural to go through the strings rapidly. This example is from the final measures of the final movement of Ravel's *Ma Mère l'Oye Suite*. It features the harp quickly going up and down the strings in glissandos. The term *gliss.* itself isn't always written but the glissando is implied with the line going between note heads.

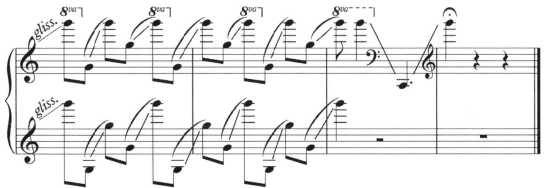

Audio Example 26.9: Ravel: Le Jardin Féérique from Ma Mère l'Oye Suite, final measures

133

One of the most popular glissandos is the opening measure of Gershwin's *Rhapsody in Blue*. This is notated as a tuplet of seventeen fast notes in a single breath.

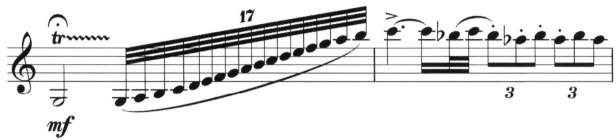

Audio Example 26.10: Gershwin: Rhapsody in Blue

Summary of Articulation

Legato = smoothly and connected

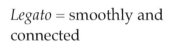

Staccato = detached and separate

Staccatissimo = very detached & disconnected

Accent

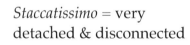

Marcato = greater accent

Tenuto = emphasis in rhythm, dynamic or both

Glissando = glide between notes

Exercises for Day 26

1. Mark these notes staccato:

2. Mark these notes legato in groups of two:

3. Mark these notes with a variety of accents:

4. Mark these notes with tenuto marks:

🦻 Listening Challenge: **What Articulation?**

In this listening challenge, you have 4 musical extracts without any articulation marks. Your task is to listen to the audio and put in all the articulation details that you can hear. *All clips are downloadable at www.schoolofcomposition.com/extras*

1.

Audio Example 26.11

2.

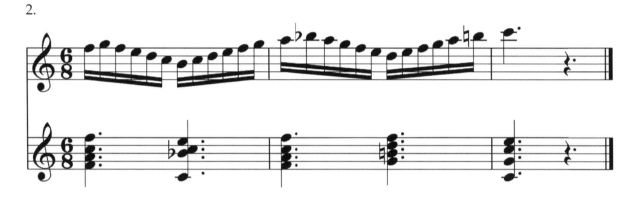

Audio Example 26.12

3.

Audio Example 26.13

4.

Audio Example 26.14

Day 27
Tempo

Tempo is the musical term for the pace of the music. As we've mentioned back in day 3, anything that has to do with time has a profound effect on the character of the music. There are hundreds of different terms for tempo in various languages, all indicating specific tempos and day 3 we learned some of the most common ones:

1. Largo – Very slow and broad;
2. Adagio – Slow;
3. Andante – At a walking pace;

4. Moderato – Moderately;
5. Allegro – Lively and fast;
6. Vivace – Very fast;

Tempo is indicated on top of the first measure of the music. The example below is marked *Allegro molto*, meaning *'Very quick'*.

Audio Example 27.1: Sibelius: Piano Sonata Op. 12

Metronome Markings

Besides the traditional terms, a metronome mark is sometimes added as well. The mark consists of two parts. What **the unit of measurement for the beat** is (whether an eighth, quarter, half note etc.) and how many **beats per minute**.

The first example below indicates that the tempo is at **80 quarter note beats per minute** while the second indicates that the tempo is at **60 half note beats per minute**.

$$\quarternote = 80 \qquad \halfnote = 60$$

In compound meters the unit of measurement is a dotted note. The metronome marking below indicates that the tempo is at **90 dotted quarter notes per minute**.

$$\quarternote. = 90$$

Sometimes metronome marks are written with the *approximately equal to* (≃ or ≈) symbol. The tempo marking here means that the music is at **around a 100 quarter note beats per minute,** giving some freedom to the performer.

$$\quarternote \approx 100$$

And this is an alternative. The letter *c.* is an abbreviation of the word *circa*, which means *approximately*.

$$\quarternote = c.100$$

On paper, the metronome mark is placed just after the tempo. It's also common for a score to have **only** the metronome marking. One of the first great composers ever to use the metronome mark was Beethoven.

Audio Example 27.2: Beethoven: 6ᵗʰ Symphony, 1ˢᵗ movement

Changes of Tempo

Once the tempo is established, music rarely remains fixed in it. Tempo changes are called for using various terms. Here we'll discuss the most common ones.

For getting slower, the terms *ritardando* (shortened *rit.* or *ritard.)* and *rallentando* (shortened *rall.)* are used. Both are Italian for *slowing down.*

Audio Example 27.3: Francisco Tarrega, Capricho Arabe, measures 31 – 35

Some argue that there are differences between these two terms but even if there are, they're extremely subtle. The interpretation of music always depends on context.

A dashed line (- - - -) can be added to the term to show exactly how long it should be applied for.

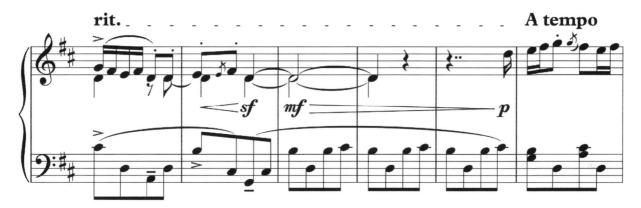

Audio Example 27.4: Bartok: Sonatina on Themes from Transylvania, SZ55, measures 19 - 25

On the other hand, the term *accelerando*, meaning *accelerating*, is used for getting faster. It is shortened as *'accel.'* and is used with or without the dashed line.

Audio Example 27.3: Francisco Tarrega, Capricho Arabe, measures 31 – 35

Just like dynamics, the words *molto* and *poco* can be added to these terms. Remember that *molto* is Italian for ***a lot*** so that ***molto accel.***, for example, means ***accelerating a lot***. On the other hand, the word *poco* is Italian for ***a little***. So ***poco rit.***, for example, means ***slowing down a little***.

Audio Example 27.5: Fauré: 3 Romances sans paroles, Op. 17, final measures

The return to normal tempo after a short change is marked by the term **A Tempo**, Italian for ***in time***. An example is in Tarrega's *Capricho Arabe* (example 27.3). **Tempo Primo** or **Tempo I** Italian for ***first (or original) time***, marks a return to the original tempo after a **longer** digression out of it as shown in example 27.6:

Audio Example 27.6: Scriabin: Sonata No. 3, 4ᵗʰ movement, measures 51 - 59

Fermatas

A *fermata*, Italian for *pause*, indicates that **the note should be held for longer than its written duration**. The symbol is half a circle with a dot.

It's also commonly referred to simply as a *pause*. Its precise duration is left up to the performer (or in the case of orchestral music, to the conductor). The pause can occur anywhere else in the music as well. In such instances, normal tempo and meter usually resume after the pause is executed. Here it is at the very beginning of the piece:

Audio Example 27.7: Schubert, 1st Impromptu, Op.90, measures 1 - 3

In this next example the fermatas are above rests so that it's the silence that is prolonged.

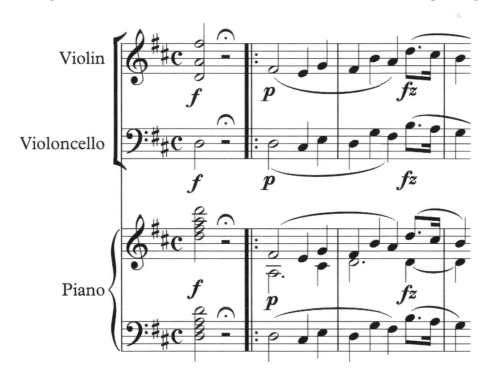

Audio Example 27.8: Haydn: Trio in D major, Hob.XV:24, 1st movement

141

And here it is written over a bar line. This indicates that a silence should be inserted between the two measures.

Audio Example 27.9: Tchaikovsky: Sleeping Beauty Suite, Op.66, Prologue, measure 43 - 45

When the music is for several instruments, the fermata sign is the same for all of them.

Audio Example 27.10: Mendelssohn: Two Concert Pieces for Clarinet and Basset Horn, Op. 113 No. 1

And finally, these are two variations of the *fermata* sign. The first indicates a shorter pause and the second indicates a longer pause:

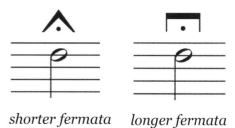

shorter fermata   longer fermata

Breath Mark

For wind instruments, the breath mark is an instruction to take a breath. For other instruments, it's interpreted as **a slight pause**. The tempo is not altered but the last note before the mark is shortened slightly to allow some space and time for catching a breath.

The symbol for the breath mark is like an apostrophe: ❯ And it's placed just above the music.

Audio Example 27.11: Debussy: Syrinx, measures 21 – 27 (flute)

Summary of Tempo Terms

Tempo Changes

Ritardando / rallentando = slowing down;
Accelerando = speeding up;
A Tempo = back to normal tempo after a change;
Tempo primo = back to the original tempo.

Pauses

Pause   Long Pause   Short Pause   Breath mark

Exercises for Day 27

1. Which one of these terms is Italian for **slow**?

   Moderato / Andante / Adagio / Vivace

2. Which one of these terms is Italian for **very fast**?

   Moderato / Andante / Adagio / Vivace

3. Which one of these terms is Italian for **at a walking pace**?

   Moderato / Andante / Adagio / Vivace

4. Mark these notes with 1 different *fermata* sign each:

5. What is the meaning of this sign? $\circ = 60$

_____

6. What is the meaning of *accelerando*?

_____

7. What is the meaning of *A Tempo*?

_____

🎧 Listening Challenge: **What's Changed in Tempo?**

In this listening challenge, you have 1 musical extract played in 4 different ways (in regards to tempo). Your task is to listen to the audio and put in all the details that you can hear. *(The clips are downloadable at www.schoolofcomposition.com/extras)*

Original (audio example: 27.12)

1.

Audio Example 27.13

2.

Audio Example 27.14

3.

Audio Example 27.15

Day 28
Bar Lines & Repeat Signs

Apart from the regular bar line, a variety of other bar lines are useful to indicate specific moments in the music.

The **final bar line** is written at the last measure, indicating that the music ends here.

 The **double bar line** indicates that there is a significant change in the music such as the beginning of a new section.

Music that is written inside the **begin repeat sign** (or 'open repeat') and **end repeat sign** (or 'close repeat') is repeated (it's played twice). Notice the dots accompanying the lines:

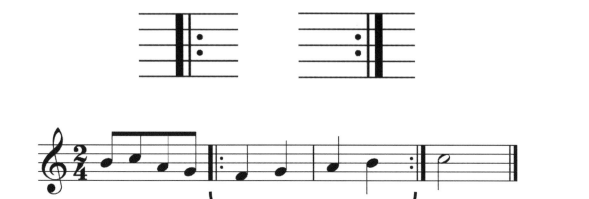

played 2 times

Audio Example 28.1

But when a section of music is repeated from the very beginning, the first repeat sign is normally left out. In this early *Minuet* by the young Mozart, the first four measures are repeated.

Audio Example 28.2: Mozart, Minuet KV1c

Upon repeating, a new ending is sometimes called for. This is notated with the **alternate ending** lines. The brackets numbered 1 and 2 below are alternate endings - once the music is repeated (as instructed by the repeat signs), the 2nd ending replaces the 1st.

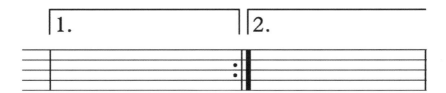

Here's a very simple example. On the first playing, the melody is played till the first ending *(measure 5)*. At this point it is repeated from the note C *(measure 2)* and the 1st ending is replaced by the 2nd ending.

Audio Example 28.3

This is how the very same melody would be written without the repeat marks:

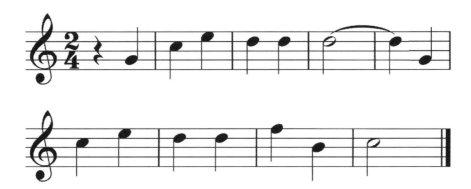

Audio Example 28.3

> *When these signs are used in actual music, they save space and make it easier to read the written music. These short examples are made up just for this lesson.*

Other Repeats

1. Da Capo al Fine

The **Da Capo al Fine** marking is an instruction for the musician to go back to the beginning and play till the measure marked **Fine**. The term *da capo al fine* is Italian for *'from the beginning to the end'*. It's often abbreviated simply as **D.C al fine.**

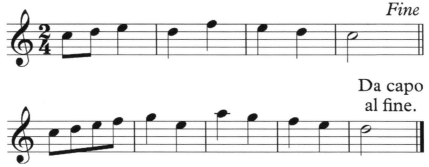

Audio Example 28.4

In the short example above the 8 measures are played in full and then the first 4 measures are played again. The music ends at the word *fine*.

2. Dal Segno al Fine

The **Dal Segno al Fine** (Italian for *'from the sign to the end'*) is related to the *da capo* but instead of repeating from the very beginning, it is an instruction to repeat from the measure marked with this sign:

The term *Dal Segno al Fine* is often shortened into **D.S. al Fine.** In this example, the melody is 16 measures long. Once the first 12 have been played, measures 5 to 8 are played again. (This is because measure 5 is where the *segno* is). The melody finishes at the word *fine*.

So the measures are played in this order: 1 to 12 – 5 to 8.

Audio Example 28.5

148

3. Da Capo al Coda

Da Capo al Coda (from the beginning to the ending) instructs the musician to go back to the beginning and play till the measure labelled *al Coda* – Italian for *to the ending*. Once there, the musician skips to the measure labelled *Coda* – a musical term for *ending*.

The *coda* itself is marked with this symbol:

In this example the melody is 16 measures long. It's first played till the term **D.C. al Coda** (measure 8). From here, the music goes back to the beginning till the term **al Coda** (measure 4). From here, the melody goes to the **coda** sign (measure 9) and is played to the end (measure 12).

So the measures are played in this order: 1 to 8, 1 to 4, 9 to 12.

Audio Example 28.6

Day 28 Quick Summary

♫ *Final bar line:*

♫ *Double bar line (for a significant change in the music):*

♫ *Repeat signs:*

♫ *Alternate endings:*

|1. ||2.

♫ *Da Capo al Fine:* from the beginning to the measure marked 'Fine'

♫ *Da Capo al Segno:* from the beginning to the measure marked with the symbol: 𝄋

♫ *Dal Segno al Coda:* from the symbol: 𝄋 to the measured marked: ⊕

149

In this listening challenge, your task is to listen to the audio and put in the correct bar lines, repeat signs and/or alternate endings to make the written music match the audio.

The clips are downloadable at www.schoolofcomposition.com/extras

1.

Moderato

Audio Example 28.6

2.

Andante

Audio Example 28.7

3.

Allegro

Audio Example 28.8

In this listening challenge your task is to find the score (available on imslp.org) of Beethoven's 11 *Bagatelles, Op. 119* and read it while listening to the music (available on YouTube & streaming services at the time of writing).

In the score, look out for several of these bar lines and repeat signs in action. Due to time constraints some performers sometimes choose to ignore repeat signs. Keep a look out for that too! Here are some suggestions as to what to pay attention to:

Bagatelle 1: alternate endings, double bar line.

Bagatelle 3: repeat signs, dal segno al coda

Bagatelle 4: alternate endings, repeat signs

Bagatelle 5: two sets of alternate endings

Bagatelle 6: two double bar lines

Bagatelle 8: simple repeat signs

Bagatelle 9: simple repeat signs

Bagatelle 10: alternate endings

Bagatelle 11: repeat signs

All the pieces, of course, end with a final bar line.

Day 29
Expression Marks for the Piano

A standard piano has 2 or 3 pedals.

The pedal that is used most is the one on the right – the **sustain pedal**. Its job is to let notes ring out (sustain) even after the piano keys have been released.

This symbol: 𝓟𝓮𝓭.   or 𝓟   instructs the player to press the pedal.

This symbol: ✳ is known as the *'release pedal'* or *'pedal up'* and it instructs the player to let go of it.

Audio Example 29.1: Rachmaninoff - Moment Musicaux Op. 16 No. 4, measure 5

This line is an alternative to the **release pedal** symbol: ‾‾‾‾‾‾‾/\

The wedge is where the pedal should be lifted (and so the sustain stopped). With the alternatives in place, the example above might be rewritten like so:

152

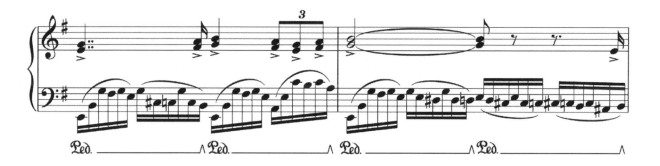

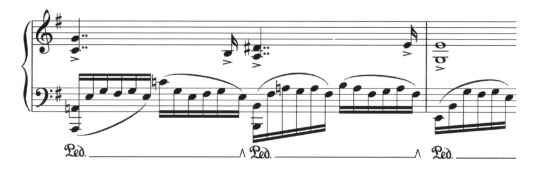

Music is sometimes marked with just one *ped.* mark in the beginning. This implies that the composer wants the sustain pedal to be used but the details of when to press and release are left up to the pianist.

So rasch wie möglich

Schumann: Grand Sonata No. 2

The left pedal is the **soft pedal** or the **una corda**. As the name implies, its job is to soften the overall timbre of the piano. Although performers employ the soft pedal at their own discretion, its use can also be specified with the words *una corda* or *due corde*.

Andantino

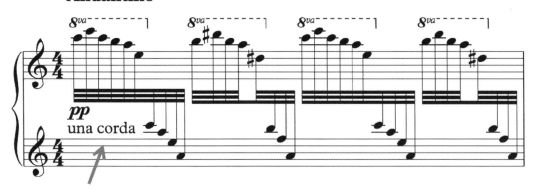

Audio Example 29.2: Saint-Saëns: Aquarium from Carnival of Animals, 1ˢᵗ piano

The release of the pedal is marked with the term ***tre corde*** (three strings) or ***tutte le corde*** (all the strings).

Audio Example 29.3: Albéniz: Suite Española, No. 4: Cadiz, measures 42 - 45

The middle pedal (not found in pianos with only two pedals) is the ***sostenuto*** pedal. The *sostenuto* pedal mechanism allows the pianist to sustain only the notes that are already depressed when the pedal is engaged. This means that a note or a chord can be sustained while the fingers move on to other notes or chords (that are not sustained).

Pianists often employ this pedal at their own discretion, but modern composers do specify its use. The term *sostenuto pedal* or *sos. ped.* instructs the player to engage it. And similar to the sustain pedal, it's released either:

1) At the ***pedal up*** symbol: ✴

2) Or at the wedge of this line: _____∧

Final Note: Second Voice Notation

When a staff holds more than one voice, the notation must be clear. **Every expression mark is written alongside the note it belongs to**:

Day 29 Quick Summary

Position	Name	Instruction to Engage	Instruction to Release
Right Pedal	Sustain Pedal	𝓟𝓮𝓭.	✳ or ____⋀
Left Pedal	Soft Pedal	'una corda' or 'due corde'	'tre corde' or 'tutte le corde'
Middle Pedal	Sostenuto Pedal	'sos. ped.'	✳ or ____⋀

Exercises for Day 29

1. Write symbols to indicate that the sustain pedal is engaged at the beginning of every measure and released at the end of every measure:

2. Make the top notes *legato* (in groups of 2 notes) and the bottom notes *staccattissimo* by adding the right articulation marks:

3. Make the top notes accented and mark the bottom notes with *tenuto* by adding the right articulation marks:

3. Make the top notes legato in groups of 2 and mark the bottom notes with *staccato* by adding the right articulation marks:

🎧 Listening Challenge: **Pedal Up or Pedal Down?**

In this challenge you'll find 3 musical extracts with 2 audio versions of each: one with the sustain pedal engaged and the other without. Your task is to listen to the audio and determine which is which. Write *'yes'* to indicate that the sustain pedal is engaged and write *'no'* to indicate that it isn't.

1.

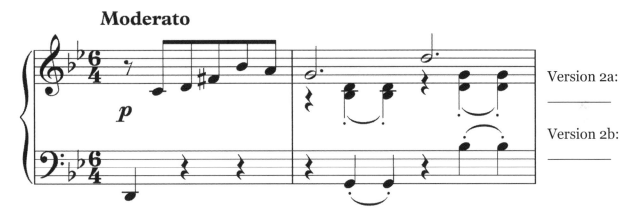

Version '1a': _____   Version '1b': _____

2.

Version 2a:

_____

Version 2b:

_____

3.

Version 3a: _____

Version 3b: _____

Score read Mikhail Glinka's *The Lark* from *Farewell to St. Petersburg* and identify as many signs and symbols as possible. Notice the effect they have on the music.

Here is the introduction of the arrangement for solo piano (by Balakirev) but it's a good idea to find the full score on *imslp.org*. Several recordings of this piece are available on streaming services as well as YouTube.

Glinka: The Lark from Farewell to St. Petersburg

Welcome to Day 30!

In these past 29 lessons we've been through a lot of material. You now have a solid foundation in musical notation and beginner music theory. Well done! The test here covers everything so if you need to revise anything at anytime, go ahead (it's perfectly normal when learning anything new). The summaries at the end of every lesson are specifically designed as a quick reference to the topic of that day.

One piece of advice: Do the test on separate sheets of paper so that you can come back to the book anytime and go over the test again without looking at what your first answers were. The answers to this test and other extras are available for download at: www.schoolofcomposition.com/extras

Day 30
Final Test

1. Why is rhythm one of the most fundamental aspects of music, even more than pitch?

2a. On a separate sheet, name and write the first 5 note values from longest to shortest.
2b. Next to your answers for 2a, write each of those note values' equivalent rests.

3. In relation to each other, the duration of these note values: *(choose only one)*

    a) is fixed;   c) depends on tempo;
    b) is always changing;   d) depends on meter;

4. In order to know exactly how long a note should be played for, we must be aware of: *(choose only one)*

    a) the tempo of the piece;   d) both meter and tempo;
    b) the meter of the piece;   e) the beats per minute on the metronome;
    c) the pulse of the music;

5. What does it mean when we say that the meter is *in three* or that it is a *triple meter? (choose only one)*

a) The rhythm repeats three times;
b) The meter is three times faster than before;
c) The strong beat occurs every three beats;

d) The time signature is specifically three-four;
e) The Bpm is a number divisible by three;

6. Meter, represented by the time signature, is essential because: *(choose two)*

        a) It tells us how many beats there are per measure;
        b) It tells us how fast the notes should be played;
        c) It tells us what type/quality of beats they are;
        d) It tells us how many notes there should be per minute;

7. Which one is the correct statement about tempo?

      a) Regardless of what the rhythm is, one beat is always played for one second of clock time so that the tempo is not too fast nor too slow.

      b) Although the values of the notes in relation to each other are always the same, tempo is important because it determines how fast or slow those notes are.

      c) Tempo is not so important because it is the meter that decides the character and mood of the rhythm.

8. Name two ways in which we can add to the duration of a note value.

9. Meters consist of beats. These beats can be: *(choose only one)*

        a) half notes;   c) dotted quarter notes;
        b) quarter notes;   d) any note value;

10a. What is the fundamental difference between simple & compound time signatures?

10b. In brief explain what duplets and triplets are.

11. Name these notes:

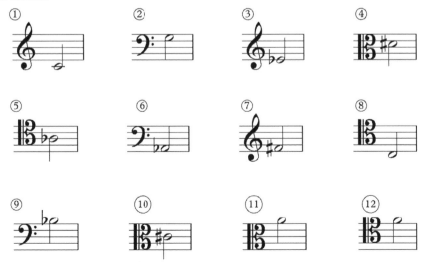

12. On a separate sheet of music paper, write these notes:

   a.   C, treble clef, half note;
   b.   D sharp, bass clef, whole note;
   c.   E flat, alto clef, quarter note;
   d.   C sharp, treble clef, quarter note;

   e.   G flat, bass clef, half note;
   f.   A natural, tenor clef, 16ᵗʰ note;
   g.   B flat, alto clef, whole note;
   h.   B natural, tenor clef, 16ᵗʰ note;

13. Write the proper clef to make these notes correct:

① E flat

② D

③ A sharp

④ G

⑤ A

⑥ D flat

⑦ C

⑧ F sharp

14. On a separate sheet of music paper, write these notes using 1 or more ledger line/s:

a. C, bass clef, quarter note;
b. A sharp, treble clef, half note;
c. B flat, alto clef, whole note;
d. G sharp, treble clef, 16ᵗʰ note;

e. D flat, bass clef, whole note;
f. G natural, tenor clef, quarter note;
g. B flat, treble clef, half note;
h. B natural, tenor clef, 16ᵗʰ note

15a. Name the given notes. In the empty measure write the note that is a half step above.

a.

b.

c.

d.
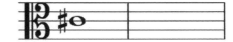

15b. On a separate sheet of music paper, write an enharmonic equivalent of your answers from question 15a.

16. Write the notes that are a whole step below the given notes.

a.

b.

c.

d.

17. How many pitches are there in our musical alphabet? And what are they named?

18. What do we mean when we say that *'this F note is an octave higher than this other F note'*?

19. What is the difference between a half step and a whole step?

20. What is the function of sharps and flats?

21. What is the name of this accidental and what does it do? ♮

22. Draw a double flat and a double sharp and explain briefly what they do.

23. Write the terms and their symbols for the 2 main dynamic marks of **loud** and **soft**.

24a. What symbol would you add on the high G notes if you wanted them to be louder (accented) than the surrounding notes?

24b. What symbol would you add to the 3rd measure if you wanted it to be **suddenly softer**?

25. Which articulation mark means **very detached and very disconnected**? _____

26. Circle the mistakes in notation of this extract *(Hint: there are eight mistakes).*

27a. How do you indicate that a piece should be played at exactly 96 quarter note beats per minute?

27b. How would you indicate that a piece should be played at around 80 quarter note beats per minute?

28. What is missing if these were the last 2 measures of a piece?

29. What does *da capo al fine* mean?

30. This symbol: ❋ instructs the player to stop depressing the sustain pedal. Which symbol instructs the player to engage the pedal?

Made in United States
Orlando, FL
23 March 2022

16046885R10093